To Rosamond

CONTENTS

FOREWORD

The four chapters that follow present with very little change the lectures as they were given in the Lent Term of 1985. A few sentences here and there and eight lines of a poem by Emily Dickinson, omitted to keep within the limits of what one can impose upon the attention of an audience, have now been restored to the text. There is always the problem, when lectures are to be published, of reconciling the very different needs of a spoken discourse, which can be smothered by too much detail, and its printed version which allows greater density and more complication of the issues. I have attempted to hold my argument to its main points, and to make as quintessential a statement as I could of what seems to me an important case.

What that case is the titles of the separate lectures ought to show plainly enough. The Clark Lectures are supposed to deal with 'some portion of English literature', and it may be objected that I have complied with this requirement in a very oblique, not to say cavalier, fashion. The reader will, I trust, recognise that the very heart of my concern is the needs and prospects of our own poetry in a time of exceptional strain and confusion. It would be rash to maintain that the morale of English poetry at the present hour is high, or that its practitioners face the future with the confidence in their art shown by that wonderfully inventive generation throughout Europe and the Americas who dominated the early and middle years of this century. We are living now in the aftermath of a great poetic era, to which the specifically English contribution was on the whole unremarkable. Nor can one disguise the fact that in the last few years many ominous signs have appeared, chief among them the rise of the so-called 'media personality'. The politics of literature and the literature of politics threaten to tear apart the fibres of a tradition sustained for more than a thousand years, and to debase one of the world's richest and most sensitive languages.

Our own poetic tradition was cradled within that of European poetry as a whole, and I wish to see that wholeness restored and with it our own place in the common endeavour. The emphasis of these lectures has indeed fallen upon only one aspect of poetry – its relation to private and public morality in the extreme circumstances of a century bringing shock after shock to the civilisation of which our grandfathers felt so assured. But as things are, and as they seem likely to continue far into the lives of our grandchildren, I believe that poetry will be called upon to play everywhere the part it has taken in Russia and generally in Eastern Europe. There is much to encourage us in what has been achieved on that side of the continent. We have need in a time of panic and evasion to strike through to some certainties. The main contention of these lectures is that poetry at its most responsible still has immense resources, and will not easily be deflected from pursuing and setting down indelibly its own form of truth.

H. G.

Bristol, April 1985

ACKNOWLEDGMENTS

I am grateful to the Master and Fellows of Trinity College not only for having invited me to give these lectures but also for the latitude they allowed in my choice of theme.

It is a pleasure to record the warmth of their welcome, and to thank particularly the Master and Lady Huxley for the hospitality shown to my wife and myself; Dr C. T. Morley, the Senior Tutor; and Adrian Poole, who with his colleagues in English Eric Griffiths and John Manrabon did much to make our visits to Cambridge so enjoyable.

In preparing the lectures I was greatly indebted to their first reader Adolf Wood, whose sensitivity and judgment I have learned over the years of our friendship to appreciate very highly, and to their first auditor, my wife, always ready to put other things aside when I asked her and to watch out for obscurities or defects of tone. I owe Margaret Milsom my thanks for the promptness and accuracy with which she typed the text. Iain White's editorial help and care have been indispensable.

CHAPTER 1

THE FUNCTION OF POETRY AT THE PRESENT TIME

Since I am embarking upon an apology for poetry, a brief personal apology may also be allowed. All my teaching life was concerned with English literature, and at a later stage to some degree with American; but most of my spare time went to the study of Russian writers – notably Pushkin and Tolstoy, with a precursor of modern poetry, Fyodor Tyutchev, and so to Blok and Pasternak. In recent years I have become greatly interested in the Russian poets contemporary with Pasternak. To hold in balance two great literatures, English and Russian, is to be made aware of important differences in their traditions, while none the less noting how manifestly they belong to a single culture. My generation, which grew up (to put it charitably) in the nineteen thirties, was plunged immediately into the divided and perplexed era that has continued to this day. We could recognise and abhor fascism, the undisputed evil at the heart of Europe. What too many of us would not concede was that the Soviet Union showed more than a few hideous parallels with Nazi Germany. But those who were drawn to Russian literature, through an original sympathy with Russian politics, did at least have the good fortune to find in it a new perspective for viewing our own literature of the time. It soon became clear that the function and status of poetry in Russia, and in Eastern Europe generally, did not correspond to their function and status as mainly understood in Western Europe and America. It was also plain that the modern poetry of Russia in particular held a growing significance for the present time, not only because of its depth and richness, but also because it seemed to speak directly to what could, sooner or later, become our own needs.

In attempting to survey some of the problems that confront poets today, I have been compelled to limit the range of enquiry. Much of what I shall say about Anglo-American poetry centres upon Eliot, and many of his statements will be familiar. On the other side (and by no means always as adversaries) Mandelstam will be often invoked, and also at times Marina Tsvetaeva, and the Russian poet nearest to him among his contemporaries, Anna Akhmatova. Beside them will appear a less likely figure, perhaps, George Seferis. He is chosen partly by reason of his own experience and that of his country, but equally because his critical writings, on a level with his poetry, are finely perceptive and bear on more than the situation of modern Greece. These are not the only poets I shall mention, but it is from them that I have learned most.

T. S. Eliot gave his Charles Eliot Norton Lectures, *The Use of Poetry and the Use of Criticism*, at a moment when the portents of violent change were visible. It was the winter of 1932–3, when Hitler came to power, Stalin had taken the decisive steps towards a personal dictatorship, and America found itself deep in crisis, turning to Franklin Roosevelt. The modern world was now set irreversibly on its course. But the process had begun earlier, as Lawrence's comment in *Kangaroo* will remind us:

2

It was in 1915 that the old world ended. In the winter 1915–1916 the spirit of the old London collapsed; the city, in some way, perished, perished from being a heart of the world, and became a vortex of broken passions, lusts, hopes, fears and horrors.

In Russia Vladimir Mayakovsky was prophesying that the year 1916 would wear revolution like a crown of thorns. His prophecy, though a little impatient in its dating, was substantially right. Much later Akhmatova was to describe how, in the last winter before the war, there drew near to St Petersburg 'the real, not the calendar, twentieth century'.

Lawrence, it must be admitted, sounds not far from hysteria, with the 'vortex of broken passions, lusts, hopes, fears and horrors'. The whole chapter in *Kangaroo* telling of his ordeal in an inimical society during wartime bears a frenzied note. And yet the calmest appraisal of events in the last seventy years cannot dispense with such terms as horror and the perishing of cities. When Matthew Arnold spoke on 'The Function of Criticism at the Present Time', it was in a time that now seems remote from our own. He could not have foreseen how much degradation and fear lay in store for the twentieth century. 'As for misery', Wilfred Owen protested in 1917 about Tennyson, 'was he ever frozen alive with dead men for comforters? [. . .] Tennyson, it seems, was always a great child. So should I have been, but for Beaumont Hamel.'

Twice in his lectures Eliot quoted Norton himself on 'a new stage of experience' that lay before mankind − this he had predicted in letters of 1869 and 1896 − and on the 'new discipline of suffering' it would impose. The suffering in this century has put an intolerable strain on the human spirit. Owen's misery in the trenches − 'frozen alive with dead men for comforters' — does not mark the furthest limit of ordeal. His conscience, he felt, was 'very seared' because he had been obliged as a soldier to disobey the teaching of 'pure Christianity'. Nevertheless, his choice to do this had been free. More terrible assaults on conscience have befallen thousands upon thousands since, not in war but in civil life. There are more paralysing fears than even Beaumont Hamel could inspire.

When Norton, and Eliot also, referred to 'our civilisation', they had in mind Western Europe and the United States. Eastern Europe for Eliot lay outside the civilisation for whose future he feared:

> Who are these hooded hordes swarming
> Over endless plains, stumbling in cracked earth,
> Ringed by the flat horizon only [. . .]

The 'hooded hordes' evoke memories of the Tatars, and perhaps of the Vandals and Huns who had preceded them. An earlier draft of this passage in *The Waste Land* had designated the plains as Polish. Eliot, the most deeply committed of English-speaking poets in his age to European values, was never willing to accord Eastern Europe an equal share in our common inheritance. This makes highly relevant another set of Charles Eliot Norton Lectures, *The Witness of Poetry*, given in 1981–2 by Czeslaw Milosz. He was born in 1911 at Vilna, 'on the very borderline', as he puts it, 'between Rome and Byzantium', though he hesitates to invoke those historical names. The West–East axis that began with the rift between the Latin and Greek Churches has persisted in Europe, but Milosz is careful to say that it 'constantly

4

takes on new forms'. He complains that until very recent days the literary map of Europe drawn in the West revealed a virtual blank from the farther side of Germany until it came to Moscow (and he might have added St Petersburg/Leningrad). For young intellectuals born like himself in those slighted regions it was a certainty, as he says in one poem, that 'the capital of the world' could only be Paris, to which Milosz himself went, as 'a young barbarian'. The catastrophes that later befell both Paris and his native Poland convinced him that everything had changed: 'There is no capital of the world, neither here [in Paris] nor anywhere else.' In his Norton lectures he turns continually to the experience of those living on the 'endless plains' as something from which poets everywhere can take their lesson.

The 'divided world' in which we are to consider the place of poetry is that surveyed by Milosz – the area once known as Christendom, with its extensions across the Atlantic. These include, if only by implication, Latin America. In the old Europe a single culture supported one religion, in its Roman and Greek forms; and, so far as poetry is concerned, that unity still prevails. There may be a tinge of parochialism in calling this a world, but what I shall have to say about it is probably not untrue on a global scale. The same conditions are beginning to show everywhere; the same drastic confrontations between an older way of life, rapidly losing its hold upon the unspeculative mass of men and women, and what is indeed 'a new stage of experience'.

I shall come back later to Milosz' views, for he raises many important issues, and much of what he has to say is borne out by my reading of Russian poetry. But first we should consider some indications of the way poetry was regarded, East and West, in the decade or so before the Second World War. At the beginning of the century it had done a great deal, through the Symbolist movement, to regain the central position in literature yielded some fifty years earlier to the prose novel. The new hegemony was not absolute, rather it might be termed a sharing of power; but the driving force — more noticeably in some literatures than in others — tended once again to be poetry. What was written by the generation of poets that made itself known around 1910 will surely stand as a remarkable achievement. And yet to hear what, within a few decades, poets were saying about the degree of public respect for their art is to encounter a sense of uneasiness and uncertainty, most of all in the West.

Robert Lowell said that in the late thirties, when he was studying at Kenyon College under John Crowe Ransom, 'no profession seemed wispier and less needed than that of the poet'. These were years of increasing political commitment, in which a serious poet of the strictest integrity, the American George Oppen, had given up writing verse for what turned out to be twenty-five years, because, he explained: 'When the crisis occurred [in 1929] we knew we didn't know what the world was [...] And I thought most of the poets didn't know about the world as a life.' The situation in America was well described by Lionel Trilling in an essay that noted the indulgence of liberal intellectuals to Theodore Dreiser and their severity towards Henry James. 'With that juxtaposition', he wrote, 'we are immediately at the dark and bloody crossroads where literature and politics meet.' Trilling's essay was entitled 'Reality in America', and this comment dates from 1946, though it was equally true of the previous decade. Radical thinking, whether in the West during the 1930s or again at the present time, or in Russia during the later nineteenth century and afterwards, has always insisted on its unique claim to interpret 'reality'. Aleksandr Blok, soon after the February revolution in 1917, asked himself the crucial question: 'Does democracy need the artist?' By democracy he meant the revolutionary movement to which Russian radicals had dedicated themselves for a century. The question invariably arises in a pressing political context; and our age lives in the grip of politics.

It is easy for poets in the West to despair of their art being taken seriously, now that the literary scene is dominated by journalism. Not long ago John Ashbery was reported as saying in an interview that 'poetry is a hopelessly minor art'. *The Times*, to console him, I should imagine, published his interview under the heading 'The major genius of a minor art'. Ashbery conceded that 'there are many more interesting things to do' than to read poetry. His diffidence (if it was that, and not simply desertion in face of the enemy) had been anticipated by an unquestionably major poet, George Seferis. *Logbook I*, the volume of verse he published in 1940, carried an epigraph from Hölderlin − the painful outcry in 'Brot und Wein' which tells of the poet's loneliness, his uncertainty about what should be said or done in a time of perpetual waiting. He is led to exclaim: '*wozu Dichter in dürftiger Zeit?*' which Seferis translated: 'And the poets, what use are they in a mean-spirited time [*s ena mikropsycho kairo*]?' *Mikropsychos* is a word used by the orators Isocrates and Demosthenes, and by Aristotle in the *Ethics*; it carries a moral weight perhaps

7

stronger than *dürftig* implies. Hölderlin in 1801 was lamenting that he could not hope to converse with the gods of Hellas: for him, as Keats would fear in 1818, it seemed too late a day to have 'touched the beautiful mythology of Greece'. Seferis, we learn from an article written in these years, rejected Hölderlin's romantic vision which did not relate to the Hellenism he understood. The question asked by Hölderlin had for him another significance. What troubled him profoundly was the lack of direction in Greece and generally in the modern world.

Seferis is a European poet necessary to know because his problems, which were those of his people, concern our common civilisation now and in the future. When he asked in the thirties what use are the poets, he seems already to have known what it should be. His own work from that time onwards gave a positive answer.

Like others in that region of Europe he had been brought early face to face with calamity. His birthplace, the Greek city of Smyrna on the Turkish mainland, was lost for ever to Hellenism in 1922 by the folly of King Constantine and his prime minister Gounaris. The 'Asia Minor disaster', as the Greeks call it, awakened Seferis to the instability of modern civilisation, and to the imperative need to define and preserve a truly Greek culture. When the liberation movement began almost two centuries ago, it had been given a voice by the poets. Solomos and Kalvos, attempting to write in the living tongue of the people, inspired the resistance much as Mickiewicz did that of the oppressed Poles. Seferis was already convinced, before he had to endure the further disasters of Greece in the Second World War, that the Greek classics could only be brought into the present through a live contemporary culture, to be found in the language of the people, the demotic, and there alone. He believed that by using this language the writer could achieve truthfulness in his work and so become genuinely Hellenic.

Vittorio Sereni, an Italian poet whose unhappy experience in Athens during 1942 as a member of the Axis occupying forces led him to the study and appreciation of Seferis, singled out a poem entitled 'The Last Day'. It had been written in Athens at the beginning of 1939, and it appears in *Logbook I*. The poem describes a day of unbroken cloud, in which none of the decisions urgently needed are made. The soldiers present arms in the drizzle, but nothing is settled of more significance than the name for the wind blowing – 'not a northeaster, the sirocco':

And yet we knew that by daybreak for us would remain
nothing more, neither the woman at our side drinking sleep,
nor the recollection that once we had been men [. . .]

The poem returns to this theme near the ending:

By daybreak for us there would remain nothing: total surrender;
        not even our hands;
and our women working for strangers at the well-heads,
        and our children
in quarries.

Sereni notes that this was written under the dictatorship of Metaxas and that it foresees the war which came to Greece the following year and also Seferis' exile. He links it with what Seferis had written elsewhere in prose about the sudden ruin of a world that had been living, its customs and rituals, and the nexus of its life. In Seferis he recognised 'an inheritance of ancestral memory that is nature and blood even more than a culture'. Hector in the *Iliad* − as Seferis' translators into English, Edmund Keeley and Philip Sherrard, point out − prophesied that his wife would one day draw water, much against her will, in another place. The quarries, they note, in which the children must labour recall those of Syracuse where Thucydides tells that the Athenian prisoners were thrown after their expedition failed in 413 B.C. These examples, of course, belong to 'culture', but supporting them is the long tradition of facing disaster which has truly become for the Greeks 'an inheritance of national memory'.

Seferis, then, made it his task, particularly in the period of exile and defeat from 1941 until 1944, to establish and repossess the tradition of Hellenism. A poem he wrote in the Transvaal among the agapanthi, alien flowers bearing a Greek name, comes near to capitulation:

> It is heavy and hard, the living do not suffice me:
> first since they do not speak, and moreover
> because I ought to question the dead
> so that I may proceed farther.

But the African lilies 'hold the dead speechless'. That was in his despair when he lost the northern constellations and with them the Hellenic world and Europe. Recovery came through lonely meditation on the Greek experience in its modern phase. He took with him to South Africa a volume of Aeschylus, he was lent the poems of Cavafy; he reflected on the forerunners of modern Greek poetry, Solomos and

Kalvos, and the restraints upon them, only half at home as they were in the living language; and he spoke movingly to his countrymen in Alexandria and Cairo about a simple hero of the Greek War of Independence, Makriyannis, the peasant who became a general and taught himself letters to write his autobiography. What made him for Seferis 'the humblest but also the most constant teacher' (even more, one suspects, than Socrates of the *Apology*) was an impersonal love of justice, and a quality he shared with the primitive painter, Theophilos – his 'intense and active culture', more valuable than any formal education. In the speech Seferis made in 1963 when receiving the Nobel Prize, he described his country as a rocky peninsula in the Mediterranean, with only three assets – the struggle of its inhabitants, the sea, and the light of the sun. Their language from ancient times had been permeated with the desire for justice and the love of humanity. Greek poetry showed this. Now at last he could affirm that in a world tyrannised by fear and disquiet there was need for poetry. 'It is', he declared, 'an act of faith'.

In the West there are not so many who would grant to poetry the significance claimed for it by Seferis. It is only, as Milosz observes, 'when an entire community is struck by misfortune' – and he instances the Nazi occupation of Poland – that 'poetry becomes as essential as bread'. Yet the belief, expressed in that very image, has found passionate adherents elsewhere. Mandelstam at a time of great personal distress affirmed it and Marina Tsvetaeva likewise; Pablo Neruda and César Vallejo use the same image. Milosz quotes a letter from Simone Weil in the summer of 1941, when France had known catastrophe: she said that 'the writers of

11

the period just ended are responsible for the miseries of our time'. The first half of our century, she maintained, was marked by 'the weakening and near disappearance of the notion of value'. Seferis described, in his lecture on Makriyannis, the main activity of European intellectuals between the two World Wars as a search for reality in life, which the moment it was touched became ashes.

Simone Weil was attacking the Dadaists and Surrealists, and her charge of moral insouciance is well founded. It could not be applied to the most influential exponent of poetry in the English-speaking world at that time, Eliot, nor to Eliot's associate and mentor at the beginning of his career, Ezra Pound. In *Lustra* (1916) Pound instructed his songs to

> Move among the lovers of perfection alone.
> Seek ever to stand in the hard Sophoclean light
> And take your wounds from it gladly.

The lovers of perfection are addressed in another poem:

> O helpless few in my country,
> O remnant enslaved!

They are 'artists, broken against her [. . .] /Lovers of beauty, starved [. . .] /You of the finer sense'. In another poem, he declares to the songs: 'Let us take up arms against this sea of stupidities.' The 'hard Sophoclean light' of Pound should not be mistaken for the illumination Seferis gained from Aeschylus. As an exile in Johannesburg, he had been overcome when reading Prometheus' invocation to 'the divine ether' and 'all-seeing circle of the sun' – first, because Prometheus is calling for justice, but also because Seferis himself had an almost mystical feeling for the Greek light. In the

12

same way as a chorale by Bach it gave him an assurance of all that was indestructible in humanity. Pound's 'hard Sophoclean light' is properly the medium for Imagist poetry (after the 'mists and fogs' since the nineties): it may wound, but only by showing the inadequacies of his art.

This declaration of Pound may seem to have more in common with Pater than the modern world, and his objectionable politics of a later period were those of a muddled man who remained primarily an aesthete. Eliot was more than that, as his religious concerns make clear. He committed himself to a lecture on 'The Social Function of Poetry' which was addressed significantly to the British-Norwegian Institute in 1943, when Norway itself had fallen into enemy hands. In it he made the claim for poetry that it performed a social function in the 'largest sense', because it could 'affect the speech and sensibility of the whole nation'. Without poetry, he believed, 'people everywhere would cease to be able to express, and consequently be able to feel, the emotions of civilised beings'. Thus for Eliot the healthy condition of poetry is at once the support and the index of a civilisation.

But is there reliable evidence that poetry, in Eliot's words, 'actually makes a difference to the society as a whole'? Pound before him had insisted that when 'the application of word to thing goes rotten', the effect upon 'thought and order', both individual and social, is disastrous. The examples of Germany and the Soviet Union in the 1930s add weight to this argument. The debasement of language, once it is used to obfuscate rather than to establish the truth, breeds cynicism. It may not be the sole cause of social decline, but it does contribute to this powerfully. Indeed the language of advertisers, of public relations and the carefully created 'image', which plays so prominent a role in the free world, has brought a new kind of insincerity into our lives, and literature is not untouched by this. Pound was speaking of literature in general, but reminded us that 'the language of prose is much less highly charged' than the language of poetry. That being granted, does society, which Eliot conceded must include all those people who are indifferent to poetry, depend for the finer tuning of its moral sensibilities on this neglected art?

He maintains that 'civilised beings' must understand their emotions in order to live fully; emotions that cannot be made articulate will die. This assertion seems to rely upon the experience of an age with which he felt more sympathy than with his own. Eliot's idea of a social function for poetry requires endorsement from a settled order that can be recognised as a civilisation, even if the ideal is often besmirched in practice.

Such a civilisation existed in England for some fifty or sixty years before the civil war, when even a lesser poet like Samuel Daniel could feel assured of his place in literature and of the value of what he did:

> I know I shall be read, among the rest,
>> So long as men speak English, and so long
> As verse and virtue shall be in request [. . .]

Those are the accents of a reasonable confidence. It makes no extravagant claims, but in that modest qualification, 'among the rest', acknowledges that the poet is one of a fraternity, which determines his standing, and also enables him to assume it.

14

Daniel in 1607 upheld a natural connection between poetry and morality: 'so long/As verse and virtue shall be in request'. Verse may meet with indifference; it has to be 'in request', freely called for. But a Christian and humanist of his day never regarded virtue as an amenity, a mere grace of civilisation. By refusing to separate verse from virtue, Daniel seeks to prove the necessity of verse. Only a dozen years before, the posthumous edition of Sidney's *Defence of Poesy* had re-affirmed the seriousness of its dealings with moral truth, inculcating as it did 'magnanimity and justice'. These qualities, one may suggest, are often glaringly absent – the first even more than the second – from the public life of the twentieth century. Is there still a prospect that poetry could restore them?

Wordsworth declared that the poet succeeds in so far as he is able 'to call forth and communicate *power*'. The idea was taken up by Hazlitt and De Quincey; it reverberates imposingly through a whole generation of poets. There is a note of melancholy in *The Prelude* when Wordsworth recognises that 'the hiding-places' of his power may in time be almost entirely closed. But, whatever his personal anxiety, the affirmation holds: poetry, for Wordsworth and for the romantic poets everywhere, is something to be measured by power. Nor can Arnold avoid this criterion when discussing Wordsworth himself or Byron or Shelley. It is not something that usually comes to mind in relation to the poetry of this age. 'Poetry', said Auden, 'makes nothing happen', even though 'it survives,/A way of happening, a mouth.'

He said this in his elegy for Yeats, who died in January 1939. Nearly three years before, some memorable words

15

were uttered by Osip Mandelstam. The place and occasion could hardly have been more incongruous; the strangeness of it all gives a solemnity to what was said.

Anna Akhmatova had gone to visit Mandelstam and his wife in Voronezh (some three hundred miles south of Moscow) where he was living in extreme poverty as an exile. For Akhmatova too the conditions of life had become almost unbearable. It was the beginning of 1936; very soon the Great Terror would paralyse the country. Neither Mandelstam nor Akhmatova now seemed to have their place among living poets. The state had prevented them from publishing any more verse in their total isolation. It was then, as his widow recalls, that Mandelstam declared 'Poetry is power' – an astonishing affirmation in the circumstances. Akhmatova bowed her head in assent. For all their hardships and dangers this remained for them indisputable. Nadezhda Mandelstam looked on the scene with wonder. 'Banished, sick, penniless and hounded', she comments, 'they still would not give up their power.' And Mandelstam, she thought, had the bearing of one who wields it. His argument was unanswerable: there must be respect for poetry when it was rewarded with punishment and death.

Shortly afterwards Akhmatova wrote a poem entitled 'Voronezh':

> And the city stands all frozen over,
> As though under glass the trees, walls, snow.
> On the crystals I walk unsurely.
> Patterned sledges waver in their course.
> And above Peter of Vorónezh are the crows,
> And poplars, and a vault of light green,

16

> Washed and dull, in the sunny motes,
> And the battle of Kulikóvo yet breathes
> From slopes of the mighty, victorious land.
> And the poplars, like glasses brought together,
> Ring out at once above us more strongly,
> As though they drank to our exultation
> At a wedding feast for a thousand guests.

Hardly less surprising than Mandelstam's assertion is the tone of Akhmatova's poem, after such a visit. In that ice-bound city where she had seen his destitution she is uplifted by a feeling of celebration, of triumph. She recalls two events in Russian history connected with Voronezh – Dimitry of the Don's victory over the Tatar horde nearby, on the field of Kulikovo, and the building there of a flotilla in the 1720s by Peter the Great. As so often in her poetry, there are allusions to Pushkin. The festive close brings to mind his account of Peter's revelling after the victory of Poltava. The 'vault of light green' recalls a 'vault of pale green' in a poem by Pushkin on the splendour and misery of St Petersburg, where 'the spirit of bondage' contrasts with harmonious architecture. There is a further hint of uneasiness in the hazards of walking over the Voronezh ice, and the wobbling of the sledges. But she must still recognise the jubilation in which nature and the city with its glorious past are at one.

Afterwards she added four lines to the poem which alter the whole perspective, by stating baldly what before she had hinted at. They could not be published until very near the end of her life:

> While in the room of the disgraced poet
> Terror and the Muse keep watch by turns.

And night sets in
That is unknowing of any dawn.

Mandelstam's 'disgrace' is *opala*, on which the lexicographer Dahl comments: 'In ancient times the imperial disfavour [*opala*] [...] involved [...] exile and utter ruin'. Akhmatova whispered those lines to her friend Lydia Chukovskaya, who wrote in her diary: 'Terror and the Muse! In these two words is the key to the life of our poets.'

Through Mandelstam particularly a tradition of public responsibility, long established in Russian literature, was brought to a new focus. His understanding of the poet's role and the depth of his commitment, though exceptional in the clarity with which he expressed them, are not unique either in Russia or elsewhere in Eastern Europe. It might be protested that Rilke, to give one outstanding example, was quite as serious in his dedication, and that he too made every sacrifice that he thought was needed. But Rilke was not tested in the same way: the terror he knew was metaphysical, not an experience imposed by other people and shared with thousands. Milosz demands of poetry what it could offer in modern Poland − 'a peculiar fusion of the individual and the historical' so that 'events burdening a whole community are perceived by the poet as touching him in a most personal manner'. The poetry of the modern age has been almost invariably lyrical. Even its longer poems usually take the form of a lyrical diary, the record of privileged moments worked into a sequence. Its triumph, of which Mandelstam gives conspicuous proof, can be found in the extension it has achieved for the lyrical mode, through being constantly aware of private experience in the light of history. I do not forget that 'History', with its inexorable demands and its dustbins for those who fail to meet them, is one of the most dangerous abstractions now at play. But the history understood by poets is seldom that which the politician invokes to vindicate his aims. A mind like Mandelstam's, when exposed to history, can attain the impersonality of great drama. His verse is in the line of Aeschylus and Shakespeare, despite all the difference of form.

Once Peter the Great had taken control of the Orthodox Church in Russia, he made, as Viktor Frank has said, 'a profound spiritual vacuum', to be filled subsequently by the writers. The true voice of conscience was to be heard in literature, from the end of the eighteenth century when the writer constituted himself spokesman of the oppressed. Frank cites the famous poem that Pushkin wrote the year after the Decembrist rising of 1825 had been put down, 'The Prophet'. Its religious intensity, he says, could scarcely have been expected from this poet, very much a man of the enlightenment in education and tastes. Pushkin takes from Isaiah his image of a seraph who appears to the poet in a desert region, touches his eyes and ears, replacing his tongue with a serpent's sting, and his heart with a live coal:

> And then God's voice called unto me:
> 'Arise, prophet, and look, and heed,
> Be possessed wholly with my will
> And, coursing over seas and land,
> Fire with the word the hearts of men'.

Frank does not exaggerate when he says that for the new class of intellectuals in Russia literature became their church. Hence the anxiety of governments, under the Tsar or the Soviets, to keep the writers in check, to mobilise them on the side of authority, to smother the fire if it burned too fiercely. And not only in Russia but throughout Eastern Europe poetry has become the spearhead of resistance. Put in the plainest terms its function is to rebuild what ideology has laid waste.

Theodor Adorno believed that the horror of Auschwitz made poetry impossible to write, and his opinion is often quoted. Earlier we find Yeats complaining that a number of English poets, and Wilfred Owen in particular, had felt bound to describe modern war in terms of passive suffering. With such an attitude, 'It is no longer possible', he argued, 'to write *The Persians*, *Agincourt*, *Chevy Chase*; some blunderer has driven his car on the wrong side of the road – that is all.' The Somme or the Holocaust – they are the same in their total destruction of any human perspective. Yeats himself could write of civil war in Ireland when it was made up of separate incidents to be recorded:

> somewhere
> A man is killed, or a house burned [. . .]
>
> Last night they trundled down the road
> That dead young soldier in his blood [. . .]

When Achilles contends with the river in the *Iliad*, he is an individual hero at war with the elemental. But when lives are annihilated in their thousands, and all sense of identity is wiped out, what can poetry do but fall silent? In the devastated areas that have been such a feature of recent

20

history, language rings hollow. The words that should denote human values are the paper money of a bankrupt community. What voices are still audible when you reap the whirlwind?

That appeared to be the situation to some poets in Poland forty years ago, and equally to poets in Germany when it came to its senses again. Ours is a century preoccupied with language, its ability to conceal thought, to set limits upon it, to hold sometimes a despotic sway over minds, or to sink into a morass of ambiguities. With a growing awareness of the subconscious, the irrational in human behaviour, and of language's complicity with these forces, the coherence of life seems to have gone. It can only be presented, as too many writers believe, in terms of the absurd. The human mind is increasingly trapped in a technology that issues its own imperatives, while the affections, the 'sympathies of men' that engaged Wordsworth, are becoming destitute.

Ezra Pound began his essay 'The Serious Artist' – one of many programmatic statements – by remarking: 'It is curious that one should be asked to rewrite Sidney's *Defence of Poesy* in the year of grace 1913.' This defence has to be made in every generation, and Pound conducted it for his time with great vigour and earnestness. He addresses the class always with ruler in hand, and we may fidget under his flow of certitudes; yet in matters of art Pound's instinct was very sure. What he demanded in the essay was 'good art', and this he explains as 'art that bears true witness'. The question of the witness that poetry bears is a large one, to be taken up later. Enough to say here that the valid testimony of someone who was there requires what Pasternak called, in relation to

21

Anna Akhmatova, 'purity of attention'. This is identified as her distinguishing quality, and what it means in action is not difficult to show.

The story is well known that she tells of standing outside the Kresty prison in Leningrad, when one of countless women forming the queue heard that she was a poet and whispered in Akhmatova's ear 'Can you describe this?' The time was that of the Great Terror; everyone, she says, spoke in whispers then. Akhmatova answered simply, 'I can'; her famous sequence called *Requiem* was the result. Thirty years earlier, before the First World War, when Akhmatova as a very young woman had been famous for her intimate love poetry, she could never have foreseen this moment. But, as the epigraph supplied much later to *Requiem* declares,

> No, not under an alien sky
> Nor under protection of alien wings,
> I was then with my own people,
> Where my people was to its misfortune.

She had every right to say in one of the poems which make up the sequence that 'her tormented mouth' uttered the cry of a hundred million. Akhmatova herself, starving, in poor clothes, penniless, an outcast, was united with all those women who could not find words for their experience, and whose names she never knew.

Requiem is a magnificent poem, because the individual voice of her suffering is so deeply conscious of the general despair. It moves majestically through the agonies and the near madness she felt herself, to close upon a vision of years to come: the snow melting like tears from the statue that might

22

one day be erected to her, the brooding of the prison dove, and the ships that pass silently down the river. This final image has an effect not unlike that of the spear-grass 'by mist and silent raindrops silvered o'er' on the mind of the narrator in Wordsworth's *The Ruined Cottage*, after he has witnessed the afflictions of Margaret which are now ended: it is 'an image of tranquillity'. Akhmatova vows not to forget the rumbling of the Black Marias, the sound of the door slammed shut, and the old woman who 'howled like a wounded beast'. The pain is indelible; she feels the duty to recall it even on her deathbed; but life continues with the spring thaw, the returning dove, and the ships that can move out to the open sea.

It has always been the function of poetry at its best to describe, to put on record, what the many feel but cannot understand or articulate. The experience of Russian poets over the last seventy or eighty years made this a compelling need. It called for an extreme honesty – 'the art that is most precise' wanted by Pound – and a fulness of response which are nothing new in Russian literature. As we saw, for two centuries now its writers have borne a heavy responsibility. All through the nineteenth century there was a fierce argument among the writers themselves and the critics who often lectured them in the name of society, on their obligation to bring Russia to a more profound consciousness of itself. They were exhorted to spread the idea of liberty among the people; to advance the revolutionary struggle, or to celebrate national pride; to define the positive hero; to protest 'we cannot live in this way'. The twentieth century has raised these issues for them to a cruel degree; and the poets have been in the front line, with disastrous consequences for many. The cost of

23

integrity has been very high; but the forfeiture of it is ruinous. So the idea of witness has recovered for our time much of its religious meaning. The poet is one who testifies to the truth, if necessary with his life. As Octavio Paz has said, writing on Solzhenitsyn: 'In a century of false testimonies, a writer becomes the witness to man.' Mandelstam saw his own destiny in this light; he deliberately prepared himself for death, showing the courage that revolutionary idealists had shown before him, but with a fulness of humanity that was seldom theirs. Mandelstam's poetic career constitutes what his countrymen call a *podvig*, a spiritual feat or act of heroism, for the general good.

In a divided world, with mounting antagonisms and the decay of mutual understanding, the good faith of poetry is indispensable. On the reliability of its witness we have to depend for communication with the past and service to the future.

CHAPTER 2

THE NATURE AND VALIDITY OF POETIC WITNESS

Constantine Cavafy was an exceptionally timid man. Even to meet admirers of his poetry caused him distress: he would postpone seeing them with desperate excuses. In his daily life he was often accused of insincerity; but Seferis, having noted the fact, goes on to say: 'as a poet he appears to have been condemned to the truth, his truth, on pain of death'. That is what distinguishes the witness borne by a poet in its purest form: the necessity at whatever cost of delivering the truth as he knows it. Much of Cavafy's most important verse — on persons, events and situations in that Hellenistic and Byzantine world which had very nearly dropped out of history — may seem to bear upon the predicaments of his age in a very oblique fashion. Yet to him could be applied the precept of Emily Dickinson: 'Tell all the Truth but tell it slant.' The message is given in code, but having been mastered it presents a view of Cavafy's people, of their actualities in the light of the past, which is moving and direct. Cavafy writes in a spare, prosaic style: the very flatness of expression, the un-musicality even, are the signs of a painful effort to be sincere. In the contemplation of history he could find the right understanding of the modern world and of his place in it.

25

The truth for Cavafy, as for any poet, had to be his truth. When we say that poetry will not yield to paraphrase, that the words of a perfected poem are immutable, it must be that we recognise its truth as expressed in a unique relation between the man or woman and the given circumstances. The poem achieves a record of the experience realised as poetry. It is in one sense immediate – that is to say, it comes upon the listener or reader with the shock of a thing intensely actual – but it has done this through the mediation of the poetic process. Every new poem has been determined in a local context by the practice hitherto of its author, and in an infinitely wider one, with more profound effect, by the poetic tradition that both gave and restricted its opportunities. Until the poem has come out right, the author cannot be certain what his truth is. In a famous figure Mandelstam compares the making of poetry with the attempt to cross a river by leaping from one Chinese junk to another, each having a separate movement, an independent course.

This commerce with language, used in a particular way, is what gives poetic witness its special character. One is led to suppose, for many poets have said this, that the words and images, until their articulation in final form, cannot be received and secured except under the direction of rhythm. Thus the act of witnessing is more properly described as a listening. The inner ear of the poet is first awakened to an insistent rhythm, an emerging pattern of sound through which his perceptions, as yet unformulated, will find their relation to one another. The effort of discovering the words to fulfil this rhythmic need calls for unremitting attention. The mind is concentrated on a signal that almost eludes it, as the words

26

seem to be within grasp and these, if they are seized, may still prove to have made only an approximation to what was meant. The full meaning, as I have said, is not evident until the poet's ear is satisfied and his poem complete.

We are confronted, then, with the poet's truth, won by submission to the discipline of his art. When he obeys it perfectly, with the receptivity and control this demands, the result is an act of witness upon oath. It rests on fidelity to the language, which has to respect the common experience. And it is valid as testimony because the reader is convinced of its rightness. As Mandelstam declared: 'The consciousness of itself as being right is the most precious thing of all about poetry.'

The 'rightness' of poetry is not to be confused with the 'correctness' of party dogma, as Mayakovsky and other poets in the Soviet era found to their discomfort. (But we can hardly endorse the heady opinion of one Russian poet who said in 1936: 'The poet is always right. The politician may be mistaken, but the poet never.') 'A dogmatist in religion', Isaac Watts is quoted in Johnson's Dictionary as saying, 'is not a great way off from a bigot, and is in high danger of growing up to be a bloody persecutor.' Dogma has to be supported by the authority of sect or party. Poetic statement is challenged by every reader that comes to it. On his assent, now and in the future, its rightness depends for recognition. It needs to have its residence permit in the living world renewed as one generation succeeds another. But rightness will in the end prevail over all the changes of fashion or failures of attention.

Our concern is with the quality of witness attained by European and American poets in a cruelly testing age. Hardy in 1915, remembering Jeremiah, called his time one of 'the breaking of nations'. We have since seen on a scale almost beyond belief the breaking of human lives, of established continuities, of trust between individuals. In such a crisis the enunciation of poetic truth is not common. Its ideal balance between seriousness and play, tragic awareness and delight in living, eludes all but the strongest. A falsifying of the record can take place when good poets are coerced, or demoralised, or seek refuge in triviality and self-indulgence. But those who maintain their nerve and keep true to conscience are likely to achieve poetry of enduring power. To quote Mandelstam once more,

> silent work silvers
> The iron plough and versifier's voice.

Modern poetry, as the critic Yury Tynyanov observed in regard to one of its more teasing practitioners, the Futurist Khlebnikov, has an ethical foundation in the method it uses. This he defined as the combining of two qualities '*attention* and *fearlessness*, attention to the "fortuitous" (which is in fact the characteristic and real) [. . .], fearlessness of the word that is necessary and irreplaceable [. . .]' It is above all a capacity to note and respond to the unexpected that gives the poet his assurance:

> Now, whether it were by peculiar grace,
> A leading from above, a something given,
> Yet it befell, that, in this lonely place,
> When I with these untoward thoughts had striven,
> Beside a pool bare to the eye of heaven
> I saw a Man before me unawares [. . .]

28

There could be no more precise a statement of the way in which insight comes to the poet. The virtue of the whole passage lies in the last word quoted here, 'unawares'; but Wordsworth would not have been fully receptive were it not for the condition of loneliness. Nor would he have grasped immediately the importance of his chance encounter with the old man gathering leeches, and the 'peculiar grace' which had afforded it, if his thoughts until that moment had not been perplexed and painful. He looked up to find the man there, 'beside a pool bare to the eye of heaven'. So the mind is suddenly released from its thwarting anxieties into the pure light of vision, as though a space had been cleared for it. The triple rhyme here sets up the co-ordinates: *given* as opposed to *striven* (though it would not have been given without the striving beforehand); 'the eye of *heaven*', or the seeing by grace which is the mark of poetic witness.

'I saw a Man before me unawares [. . .]' The poet did not merely see a man; he saw a man before him, presented for his attention. We know from his sister's *Journal* that Wordsworth was not alone when he met the old leech-gatherer. The incident has been transformed into a profound visionary experience, enacted in the depths of the poet's mind as he narrates it. He has indeed put his own construction on what he saw, yet in that solitude which his imagination has claimed for itself Wordsworth is enabled to recognise with the most poignant simplicity what lies ahead of him. The old man says of the leeches that had provided his living: 'Once I could meet with them on every side.' In 1802, when Wordsworth wrote this poem, his powers were

29

still at their height. But in *The Prelude* of 1805–6 already he could expect the failing of those powers:

> I see by glimpses now; when age comes on,
> May scarcely see at all [. . .]

The poetic experience he records in the passage we have been considering is deeply engaged with the difficulties of his vocation. For poets since Wordsworth's day the most serious problem has been how to sustain their advance from one decade to the next. There is surely an undertone of envy to be caught in Eliot's comment on 'the last and greatest canto' of the *Paradiso*, where he feels Dante has achieved 'the real right thing' and displays 'the utmost power of the poet'. Henry James, so avid of 'the real right thing' – it was his phrase – questioned whether he had ever achieved it himself when the outbreak of the First World War made all his work seem irrelevant – 'The picture of little private adventures simply fades away.' The shock of great wars and upheaval on many sides has compounded the disadvantages of the modern poet. Wordsworth may have lamented the passing away of 'a glory from the earth', the decline of visionary power. But he never doubted the reality of what he had once seen. It was left for Eliot in the modern age to express a deeper unhappiness in the line from *Ash Wednesday*:

> The infirm glory of the positive hour.

Wordsworth's poem about the leech-gatherer, *Resolution and Independence*, is centred upon himself, his particular anxieties about the future. But there is also a sense in which, to varying degrees, the dictum of Eliot, following Remy de

Gourmont, holds true. 'The great poet', he said, 'in writing himself, writes his time.' On another occasion he enlarged upon this:

A poet may believe that he is expressing only his private experience; his lines may be for him only a means of talking about himself without giving himself away; yet for his readers what he has written may come to be the expression both of their own secret feelings and of the exultation or despair of a generation. He need not know what his poetry will come to mean to others; and a prophet need not understand the meaning of his prophetic utterance.

There is no reason to doubt that Eliot had his own case in mind: retrospectively he had described *The Waste Land* as 'only the relief of a personal and wholly insignificant grouse against life; it is just a piece of rhythmical grumbling'. Nonetheless, it spoke for the 'despair of a generation' throughout most of Europe. The occurrence was not unique; we should ask ourselves how this comes about.

Russian poets in the twentieth century have not shared Eliot's fear of giving himself away. Pasternak takes the opposite stance in one of his last poems when he declares: 'The aim of creating is the giving of oneself.' In this he agrees with Aleksandr Blok, who insisted on the sacrificial aspect of art, its annihilating of the personal life. Blok too, like Eliot, maintained that 'the passion [. . .] of any poet is steeped in the spirit of the age' (note that he prefers the bold term 'passion' to Eliot's discreet 'private experience'). For Blok the essential task of a poet was to reveal in his verse the rhythm of the historical moment. 'To know *his own* rhythm' was the poet's 'most reliable shield from all abuse and praise'; to lose that rhythm, his greatest calamity. In the first year of the

31

Bolshevik regime he wrote a long essay on Catiline, which he called 'A page from the history of world Revolution'. The plausibility of Blok's thesis about this political adventurer (in whom he had become interested after reading the early play by Ibsen, *Catiline*) need not be examined here. What concerns us is the relation he suggested between a poem by Catullus, the *Attis*, about the self-mutilation of a worshipper of Cybele, and the conspiracy headed by Catiline, 'the Roman Bolshevik'. Catullus' elaborately phrased poem (as Alexandrian a work as he ever wrote) is set in a complicated metre, galliambics, used by worshippers of Cybele in their chants. Blok believed that he could hear in its rhythm 'the uneven, hurrying step of a doomed man, the step of a revolutionary'. 'The *Attis*', he maintained, 'is the work of one living in a Rome rent by civil war.' It may or may not be true that Catullus's poem reflects that crisis. Blok in his essay (which another Symbolist, Andrey Bely, described as 'a dramatic poem') was celebrating what he had himself achieved in *The Twelve* a few months before. That indisputable dramatic poem marked a final escape from confinement in the lyrical mode. He could now assert that 'in a poet's sense of the world there is no gulf between the personal and the general'.

In April 1917 Blok had recognised his appointment 'by the will of fate' to be 'the witness of a great epoch'. (It was then that the question came to him, 'Does democracy need the poet?') For the previous year, on service with the Pioneer Corps behind the lines, he had written no poetry. This silence continued until January 1918 when in a matter of days he composed the 335 lines that make up *The Twelve*. It was followed by an overtly political poem, *The Scythians*, challenging Western Europe in a last appeal to unite with Russia and the East, or else be destroyed. He also wrote a prose manifesto, *The Intelligentsia and the Revolution*. But the essential statement appears in *The Twelve*, which he modestly claimed to be his one work of genius.

Blok confessed at the moment of accepting his role as a witness that he 'had no clear view of what was going on'. His diary and notebooks in that revolutionary spring and summer of 1917 show an extremely sensitive and honest mind attempting to read the time as it really was, facing doubts and a sense of personal inadequacy, and aware of momentous change in an unknown direction. Blok was the contemporary of Rilke, and in some ways might appear to have been his spiritual brother. Like Rilke he was a poet of the inward eye, mystical but ill at ease with Christianity. At every step he too remained the artist, unswerving in purpose and true to himself. But also there are differences. As a Russian poet in those years, Blok could not retire into the sanctuary of his art: a Duino or a Château de Muzot – even a Thoor Ballylee – was unthinkable for him. More than any other Symbolist of that generation in Russia, he wanted to make his art necessary to the people. Blok's tribute of 1908 to Tolstoy, whom he saw as a moral support for the whole nation, and especially for its writers, in the face of darkest reaction, indirectly acknowledges his own responsibility. For a decade before *The Twelve* he had been wrestling with these problems of conscience, seeking to understand the nature of his bond with Russia and to overcome the mutual incomprehension of the educated and the masses. Had it not been for this long and often frustrating search, he could never have concentrated his vision with such finality in *The Twelve* – a masterpiece shaped by the whole tendency of his previous work, as if from a logical necessity.

The Intelligentsia and the Revolution, of the same time as *The Twelve*, calls upon intellectuals to put aside their prejudices:

The daimon once bade Socrates listen to the spirit of music.
  With all your body, all your heart, all your awareness – listen to the Revolution!

Blok himself had undergone the strange experience, a few days before he started on his poem, of seeming to hear a continuous rumble, as of an earthquake. For him the revolution took on the elemental form of a torrent or blizzard, which shows no respect for the lives of individual men and women. So in *The Twelve* a blizzard sweeps through darkened Petrograd, the city that Pushkin had celebrated for its classical splendours in the prologue to his poem *The Bronze Horseman*. But in *The Twelve* that order has broken down. Pushkin described the 'sovereign flow' of the Neva, which later bears down in terrifying power to flood the city. The twelve Red Guards in Blok's poem march with 'sovereign tread', and they are as lawless as the river. The wind's fury accords with their 'black rage, holy rage'. The liberty they proclaim is mob rule – incendiarism, plunder, the breaking open of cellars, and the action of the poem revolves round a casual murder, when one of them shoots the girl he has loved as she careers past with his rival in a sledge. The incident is part of the anarchic terror which they uphold, admonishing one another to keep revolutionary discipline.

Why did Blok need to record this one incident, a sordid mischance, after having accepted it as his duty to be 'the witness of a great epoch'? And what dictated the extraordinary climax of his poem, in which none other than Christ, with a red flag in his hands and wearing a halo of white roses, leads the patrol?

This however was the 'clear view of what is going on' that eventually came to Blok, and in recording it he found the 'voice' that seemed to have deserted him even before the February revolution. There can be no doubt that during the days he was working on *The Twelve* Blok was caught up in a creative frenzy. His ears were filled with the music of the elements, and also with the human voices to be heard on the streets, which he noted sharply in all their confusion, and with a continual shifting of tone. Blok had always been a musical poet, and here, most unexpectedly, he had devised the harmonic scale of a new era. It was truly the first poem to make a profound response to the revolution, and to express what Russian critics would call its 'pathos' − its emotional content − with extraordinary power. *The Twelve* is poetic witness in as compelling a form as it can ever take. What then of its validity?

Only a year after Blok's death, one of his most perceptive critics, Viktor Zhirmunsky, wrote what is still among the best accounts of his poetry. He considers Blok to be 'the last romantic poet', and views his life in terms of 'a religious tragedy'. *The Twelve*, he maintains − and no critic has disputed this − brings together all that had previously been essential in Blok's poetry. There was in Blok, as in Dostoevsky, a passion for extremes, or 'spiritual maximalism' as

35

Zhirmunsky calls it; and he felt irresistibly drawn to the element of popular revolt, a spontaneous uprising which answered to his own temperament, and which he saw as terrible and pitiless, but justified by the offences of his own class. Blok did not seek, as Mayakovsky did, to become the tribune of the revolution; his duty was to accept and to record. Zhirmunsky points out that *The Twelve* does not conceal the depth of suffering that the revolution caused, or the hopelessness of a situation which offered no way out.

At the time of writing Zhirmunsky could not have seen Blok's diaries and notebooks, which bear out his argument. They show little conception of what the Bolsheviks really stood for. In July 1917 he confesses to being attracted by 'the fogs of bolshevism and anarchism'. He associated the revolutionary peasant with Rasputin, of whom he had observed earlier 'Grishka sits in me', and he thought that the sensuality of Rasputin could be found not only in himself but in bolshevism too − a grotesque error of judgment. Bolshevism had nothing in common with the elemental forces it set out to manipulate: Lenin's revolution shattered all Blok's expectations, and left him in mute despair when he recognised it for what it was.

However, the testimony of *The Twelve* is not necessarily impaired by lack of political sagacity. What he shows in the poem is closely related to impressions set down in his diary. The experience of those first revolutionary weeks would appear to have been very much of the order that Blok describes in his poem. The Red Guards of *The Twelve* repeat some political slogans of the time; their talk of 'control' (using the un-Russian word *kontrol'*) and of vigilance against the class enemy may derive from Bolshevism. But there is another dimension to their thinking too. Mandelstam noticed how much of the poem was 'drawn directly from folklore'. The proletarians of Petrograd still in many ways resembled their village ancestors, and their idea of revolution retained a colouring from memories of Pugachov in the eighteenth century and Razin in the seventeenth. Sergey Hackel made an important point when he drew attention to the spelling of 'Jesus' at the very end of the poem, which adopts the form used by the Old Believers or schismatics, who would not accept the changes in ritual and the liturgy adopted by the Russian Orthodox Church in the seventeenth century. The vast majority of them were peasants. These were the people who supported the Socialist Revolutionaries, many of whose leaders and party members eventually joined the emigration.

Blok's contemporaries, on either side in the revolutionary crisis, did not understand or welcome the appearance of Christ at the poem's conclusion. Nor was Blok easy about it, as he confessed more than once. Yet, as his diary states,

> I simply noted a fact: if you look into the columns of the blizzard *on this road*, then you will see 'Jesus Christ'. But sometimes I myself abhor this effeminate phantom.

The image of Christ, with his 'delicate step above the snowstorm', may have been influenced a little by his reading, not long before, of Renan's *Vie de Jésus*. And it is a commonplace of criticism now that it can be traced back through various metamorphoses in Blok's poetry to his original cult of the Most Beautiful Lady, who strongly resembles Sophia, or the

Eternal Feminine, as disclosed to the religious thinker Vladimir Solovyov. More interesting is the relation of Christ to the poem itself, where His way is prepared both by the Red Guards' abjuration of the cross and their inconsistent moments of prayer – 'Lord, have mercy', 'Grant peace, O Lord, unto the soul of Thy servant' (Petka's supplication for the girl he has murdered) – and also by the triumphant march of the rhythms. Christ cannot be removed from *The Twelve*.

Nor was Blok ready to yield anything. He made his final comment in April 1920:

I do not renounce what was written then, because it was written in harmony with the elemental [. . .]

And, he explained, this had been done

in that exceptional and always brief time when a revolutionary cyclone rushing by produces a storm in every sea – politics, life and literature. [. . .] I looked at the rainbow when I wrote *The Twelve*; that is why a drop of politics was left in the poem.

Zhirmunsky says that Blok's 'uprightness before himself and his contemporaries' was the service he performed as a poet of the revolution (rather than a revolutionist poet). He did not disguise from himself the tragic contradictions. As he was to observe a year later, 'a *tragic* outlook' is 'alone able to give the key to understanding the complexity of the world'.

This brings to mind the well-known declaration of Yeats: 'We begin to live when we have conceived life as tragedy.' Between Blok, 'the last romantic poet' of Russia, and Yeats, who placed himself among 'the last romantics', there are both affinities and opposition. Yeats was fifteen years older than

Blok, and outlived Blok, who died in 1921, by another eighteen years. Both were poets who evolved towards what Yeats called 'responsibilities'; each of them dominated the poetry of his nation, and brooded much upon the nation's history and its future. Eliot has described Yeats in terms that apply no less to Blok. He admired Yeats for 'an exceptional honesty and courage', in facing the need for 'adaptation to the years'. This poet represented in Eliot's view 'what I have called Character of the Artist: a kind of moral, as well as intellectual, excellence.' Blok's integrity was never in question. As to intellectual excellence, he stands below Vyacheslav Ivanov and Andrey Bely among the Symbolists, though he certainly had self-knowledge and could not be called a creature of moods. His passion for extremes did not exclude a strong sense of irony. But the intellectual vigour of Yeats (not quite the same thing as excellence) was unmistakable. It shows in various ways: his impressive control of syntax, to name one; or again the energy with which he elaborated a system to interpret history in cyclical terms. However, the honesty of Yeats − his courage is not in doubt − revealed itself in some of his concerns more obviously than in others.

When already famous, and no longer, one would have supposed, open to change, he allowed Ezra Pound to help him escape from the Celtic mists into the hard light of day. This maturing in art, which Eliot praises as 'honesty with oneself', is of course remarkable. But Yeats continued to be a master of self-reference, always aware of his posture in the poem. And for that he is blamed by a critic severe with him to the point of impatience, C. H. Sisson, who has accused him of 'cutting a figure even after his death' in the epitaph he wrote for himself:

> *Cast a cold eye*
> *On life, on death.*
> *Horseman, pass by!*

He draws attention to the egotism that obliged Yeats to overact his part, and let him see others as his own preconceptions would have them. Sisson grants that in *Last Poems* he was 'trying desperately to cast aside pretences and get to the root of his mind'. But in Sisson's judgment he was seldom free from striking an attitude.

It would not be easy to deny the charge, and for so tiresome a habit − Sisson finds it exasperating − the reason is not far to seek. Like Blok, he was passionately involved with his country, and like him uncomfortably aware of not being at one with its people. Blok's difficulty was that of the estranged intellectual and 'repentant nobleman'; but the Russia he loved and hated in no important way differed from the Russia the people knew. It may seem extraordinary that Blok, the son and grandson of professors, could have become in *The Twelve* so intimate with the idiom of the Petrograd streets, or that Mandelstam could find in Anna Akhmatova, 'a Russian literary lady of the twentieth century', the emotional timbre of a peasant woman, as her affinities with popular song brought out. The problem for Yeats lay in his being neither a Catholic nor a Gaelic speaker. He could not encounter Irish mythology in its own language; and this put a strain on his identification with an Ireland outside the Protestant Ascendancy. He liked to imagine a natural bond between noble

40

and peasant (promoting himself to the aristocracy); but the tradition of Anglo-Irish landlords was a separate one, and Yeats spent a great deal of energy on giving it form and lustre:

> I declare this tower is my symbol; I declare
> This winding, gyring, spiring treadmill of a stair
>   is my ancestral stair;
> That Goldsmith and the Dean, Berkeley and Burke
>   have travelled there.

This is 'high talk'. He glorified 'that one Irish century that escaped from darkness and confusion' − the century of those four Yeatsian heroes − in the attempt to create a mythology for his kind. The affirmation 'I declare' has the proud ring of his egotism. 'I, the poet William Yeats' has flourished a fine pedigree; but are they in any true sense his spiritual forebears?

He did gain one advantage over his English contemporaries (other than the poets of the First World War) in being brought sooner to face the issues dominating this century. It was necessary to understand that politics could become lethal and the poet had no right of immunity. At the time of Queen Victoria's Diamond Jubilee in 1897, riots broke out in Dublin. He tells of reading about the violence on the following day:

I count the links in the chain of responsibility, run them across my fingers, and wonder if any link there is from my workshop.

This anticipates the troubled note in one of his *Last Poems*:

> Did that play of mine send out
> Certain men the English shot?
> Did words of mine put too great strain

On that woman's reeling brain?
Could my spoken words have checked
That whereby a house lay wrecked?

Whatever the truth in these particular instances, he does ask a real question. Poetry when it finds a receptive audience at such times of tension can be very potent. Often in these circumstances the greater its potency, the more flagrantly does the poet betray his true function.

About Yeats's political stance in later years Conor Cruise O'Brien has written:

The political man had his cautious understanding with fascism, the diplomatic relation to a great force; the poet conveyed the nature of the force, the dimension of the tragedy.

The distinction is just, and Yeats's full poetic response to the 'violence and fear' of the age should not be confused with his direct political utterances, even when these were made in verse. O'Brien maintains that the poetry in 'Leda and the Swan' which he has been considering is concentrated 'in metaphors of such power that they thrust aside all calculated intent'. There are two things to be said on this observation. The first is that, in the final poem of 'Nineteen Hundred and Nineteen', for example, in which Yeats denounces the spreading of violence as 'evil gathers head', he seems not only appalled by the 'thunder of feet, tumult of images', but fascinated by it. In another poem of that period, 'Ancestral Houses', he speculates whether the greatness of the ancestors who built them could be admired without some respect for their violence:

> ... maybe the great grandson of that house,
> For all its bronze and marble,'s but a mouse.

Mention of 'Ancestral Houses' leads to my second point. In much of his later work a 'calculated intent' is too clearly visible. 'What is rhetoric', he once asked, 'but the will trying to do the work of the imagination?' He was thinking of French dramatic poetry, but it could also be his own problem. 'The Municipal Gallery Revisited', a poem from his final period, illustrates this. He is seeking there to evaluate 'the images of thirty years', tracing Ireland's history in the lineaments of his friends. Among the portraits that hang in the gallery is one of Lady Gregory by Mancini:

> 'Greatest since Rembrandt', according to John Synge.

Yeats feels bound to demur – 'A great ebullient portrait certainly', he says, and then proceeds to outdo Synge in extravagance:

> But where is the brush that could show anything
> Of all that pride and that humility?

Elsewhere his excitement proves too much for him:

> Heart-smitten with emotion I sink down,
> My heart recovering with covered eyes.

'The Municipal Gallery Revisited' does not seem to achieve the truth that is incontestably there in *The Twelve*. Had Yeats's position in Irish life been more secure – despite the membership of the Senate bestowed on him as the 'public man' – he could have borne witness more freely. But the impulse to aggrandise the order he cherished permits him to use for this end a masterful rhetoric. He is too often an interested

party, so that his poems impress by their beautiful con-
trivance, but are not wholly to be relied on as testimony.

Somewhere in *The Pisan Cantos* Ezra Pound compares
Yeats and Ford Madox Ford as talkers. They were both of
them friends whom he recalls with affection, and he decides
that

> old Ford's conversation was better,
>   consisting in *res* non *verba*,
>   despite William's anecdotes, in that Fordie
>   never dented an idea for a phrase's sake.

Pound himself was much concerned with things and the exact
words for them. He too, it is right to say, 'never dented an
idea for a phrase's sake'; but he could not prevent ideas from
denting his own poetry.

To judge Pound with complete fairness still remains difficult. Even the best passages in the *Cantos* are liable to
be threaded with propaganda, and the poet who among all
his contemporaries writing in English had the most perceptive ear may suddenly lapse into crudities of invective. The
Cantos which occupied him for fifty years of his working
life are Pound's attempt to reconstruct a civilisation, from
his knowledge of Renaissance Italy, the United States of
Thomas Jefferson and John Adams, and the long history
of China. He intended a cure for our present civilisation,
which he regarded as built upon usury and sustained by
the lies of democratic politicians. Where these beliefs led
him finally is, of course, notorious. His broadcasts to
America from Rome during the Second World War, ill-
judged and offensive as they were, may be discounted for our

purposes. As Samuel Johnson said firmly of a contemporary poet whose politics he disliked, 'my business is with his poetry'.

The Pisan Cantos were written when he was held in a prison cage by the United States army, awaiting indictment for treason at home. Until that moment Pound seems to have had more opinions than experience; now he needed to examine his life and its consequences both for himself and others. In these cantos a more intimate tone is often heard. There is self-reproach, for lack of compassion: 'I have been hard as youth sixty years', and when he did show pity, it was '*probablement pas assez*, and at moments that suited my own convenience'. In 1945, 'a man on whom the sun has gone down', he contemplates the ruins of the Europe he had adopted as his own, and looks back regretfully to the time in London before the first war when indeed, to quote Eliot's tribute, he had taught 'the lesson to care unselfishly for the art one serves'. The cantos are also graced with touches of simple humanity, as when he writes of his Negro captors – Mr Edwards, who said 'doan you tell no one/I made you that table', or

> Mr G. Scott whistling Lili Marlene
> with positively less musical talent
> than that of any other man of colour
> whom I have ever encountered
> but with bonhomie and good humour [. . .]

And often we note that Pound, who had generally revealed himself by indirect means – through adopting personae, through quotation, or as a translator – now speaks in his own voice of what he experiences at the moment:

The moon has a swollen cheek
and when the morning sun lit up the shelves and battalions
of the West, cloud over cloud
                        Old Ez folded his blankets
Neither Eos nor Hesperus has suffered wrong at my hands

The difficulty for Pound, as he expressed it later in a draft of Canto CXVI, was

> To confess wrong without losing rightness.

In that canto he admits

> my errors and wrecks lie about me.
> And I am not a demigod,
> I cannot make it cohere.

The *Drafts and Fragments*, published in 1970 when it had become clear to him that the mighty work must lie for ever unfinished, show a purity of regret, a more humble self-knowledge (though even here he has been toying with a comparison of himself and the demigod Herakles) that scarcely enter *The Pisan Cantos*. True, these carry the often quoted meditation on human vanity that begins 'What thou lov'st well remains [. . .]':

> Pull down thy vanity
>   How mean thy hates
> Fostered in falsity,
>   Pull down thy vanity,
> Rathe to destroy, niggard in charity [. . .]

It can be taken as an indictment of mankind in general, but on this occasion he surely would not exempt himself from the censure. He had been arrogant, his own hatreds 'fostered in falsity', he had been too quick to destroy, and he would confess in Canto CXVI,

> Charity I have had sometimes,
> I cannot make it flow thru.

As Eliot once remarked, Pound's 'hells are for other people', though it would only be fair to add that in his final years of self-imposed silence and deep contrition he knew hell for himself.

What disappoints in *The Pisan Cantos* is that they are flawed by his reluctance to lose a bad argument. Those of us who experienced the Second World War on the other side from Pound may be unwilling to hear that argument at all. Only in retrospect have the ugly compromises of allied victory become clear to us. It may be easier now to accept the emphatic statement he quotes at the end of Canto LXXVIII:

> there
> are
> no
> righteous
> wars

seeing it is qualified thus in a later canto:

> that is, perfectly right on one side or the other
> total right on either side of the battle line.

But there is some special pleading at the very end of the poem, in his conversation with the sister of the girl swineherd. He asks her to comment on the behaviour of American troops in Italy. Is it good? Scarcely, she tells him – *poco, poco*. Worse than the Germans? She replies *'uguale'* –

much the same − 'through the barbed wire'. In her own limited experience the woman could be right. Placed where it is, the statement begs an intolerably large question.

> What thou lov'st well remains
> ⁻the rest is dross [. . .]

Pound loved 'scaled invention' and 'true artistry'. It was his pride

> To have gathered from the air a live tradition
> or from a fine old eye the unconquered flame.

The virtues he admires are aristocratic, and he cares for things that will endure, like the 'house of good stone/each block cut smooth and well fitting' that *usura* makes it impossible to build. In his view 'the usual subjects/of conversation between intelligent men' were

> books, arms,
> And men of unusual genius,
> Both of ancient times and our own [. . .]

But 'the rest is dross' − the scum that smelted metal throws off, foreign matter, refuse. Against the men of resolute action, like the unscrupulous Sigismondo Malatesta, tyrant of Rimini and condottiere, he sets what he dismisses as 'pejorocracy'. At the outset of *The Pisan Cantos* we are presented with

> The enormous tragedy of the dream in the peasant's
> bent shoulders.

Mussolini and his mistress have been hung 'by the heels at Milano', and the shame of it is

That maggots shd/eat the dead bullock.

I need not dwell on the outbursts of rancour he could not silence in the hour of his ordeal − the sneers at 'Churchill's return to Midas broadcast by his liary', the BBC, or the Jewish voice lisping 'it will not take uth 20 years to crwuth Mussolini'. Pound has failed to distinguish between the 'rightness' a poet cannot afford to lose, and the certitudes of political dogma. In 1963 he confessed to an interviewer that his 'feeling of certainty' in the *Cantos* had been mistaken: 'I have come too late to the consciousness of doubt'. It is sad to recall how he had insisted, fifty years before, on the artist's duty to bear true witness.

CHAPTER 3

ISOLATION AND COMMUNITY

In 1952 Eugenio Montale spoke at an international congress in Paris, devoted to the already familiar theme of 'Isolation and Communication'. His paper, entitled 'The Solitude of the Artist', came from one particularly at home with the subject. Conditions in Fascist Italy when he published his first book of poetry in 1925 had forced him to become by and large a hermetic writer, though he was also by temperament inclined that way. He seemed to himself in those days like a man living 'under a glass bell', yet feeling nonetheless 'close to something essential'. That sense of separation from others and nearness to a hidden reality was characteristic of Montale, and it determined his line of argument in this paper. 'No one in our time', he said, 'was more isolated than Kafka; and few have achieved communication as well as he did.' Montale used this striking example to support his main contention. 'The man who communicates', he believed, 'is the transcendental I concealed in us that recognises itself in others.'

This is not the moment to pause on what Montale had to say about the communicators – the media experts – whose prominence has grown much more threatening since 1952. He insisted that it is only 'the great isolated figures' of an

50

epoch who speak and communicate: 'their isolation', he asserted, 'is more illusory than real'. Montale would have found himself in full agreement with Marina Tsvetaeva's simple proposition: 'Art is an undertaking in common, performed by solitary people.' She remarked that even Mayakovsky, who claimed vociferously to speak for the whole proletarian class, was in fact 'a solitary comrade', 'the hetman of a band that does not exist, or whose real hetman is someone else'. Pasternak on the contrary, she points out, meant by 'us' not 'the attacking class' of Mayakovsky, but 'all the solitary people of all times, apart and ignorant of each other, doing the same work'. That is to say, the community of artists − to which we might add all those who attend seriously to what the artists produce.

Montale is recognised as being the finest Italian poet since another isolated man who achieved the status of a classic, Giacomo Leopardi. In the second of his Norton Lectures Czeslaw Milosz considers what his kinsman and mentor, Oscar Milosz, a poet who wrote in French, deplored as 'a schism and a misunderstanding between the poet and the great human family'. 'Poetry', Oscar Milosz maintained, 'under the influence of charming romantic minor German poets, as well as that of Edgar Poe, Baudelaire and Mallarmé, suffered a kind of impoverishment and narrowing [...]' The poet at once complained of and was flattered by his solitude. He deliberately set himself apart from the crass and hostile bourgeoisie. By the end of the nineteenth century, when Symbolism had triumphed in poetry, the rift was complete. On one side you found the artist (a term which the poet increasingly chose to describe himself). He had become in his own eyes the priest of a mystery, the supreme artificer, a being beyond good and evil. On the other side was ranged the populace, 'all those', in Yeats's contemptuous words, 'whose minds, educated alone by schoolmasters and newspapers, are without the memory of beauty and emotional subtlety'. Such an attitude was strongly condemned by Oscar Milosz who wanted to see poetry return to the people and be 'initiated [. . .] into the most profound secret of the labouring masses'.

.But in Montale's view that possibility had gone for ever. Earlier, in 1925, he had hoped for 'the creation of a tone, a language of understanding which would bind us to the crowd for whom one works unregarded [. . .]' All he could foresee however in 1952 was art developing on two distinct levels – 'a utilitarian art not unlike sport for the masses' opposed to 'true art as such, not so different from the art of the past and not easily reducible to cliché'. It was a sound prediction, at any rate for the more industrialised societies; and if it is fully realised, the effects could be pernicious both for the popular and the 'true' art. The majority of poets would not welcome this situation. We may suspect that never in recent centuries has there been poetry in Western Europe equally understood, or understood in the same way, by all the members of a community, yet this remains the cherished hope of the poet. Czeslaw Milosz could say that in his native Poland, once it had become a single community again as the result of forty years of tribulation 'it was not unusual for 150,000 copies of a book of poems to be sold out in a few hours'. This happened in 1980, when 'the division between the worker and the intellectual' was also growing less marked.

52

Isolation, as we shall see, can take various forms. Let me begin by examining the relation of two women poets to the community. Emily Dickinson in the mid nineteenth century, and Marina Tsvetaeva in the earlier part of the twentieth, were both absolute poets, for whom their life outside poetry, though painful and real in one sense, was always secondary to the main purpose of writing. A sign of total dedication to poetry is found in their letters – or any statements they made in prose – which are (at least in the mature years of both women) intense and elliptical like the poems. Each knew that she was isolated. 'Civilization – spurns – the Leopard!' Emily Dickinson's image for herself is matched by Marina Tsvetaeva's 'bristling like a captive lion'. In the same breath Tsvetaeva speaks of being

> forced out – altogether
> Into myself, a singularity of feelings.

The word I translate as 'singularity', *edinolichie*, is apparently her own coinage, and related to the term Mandelstam once used for his own position, *edinolichnik*, properly a Soviet farmer outside the collective. Mandelstam at the time (1935) was – temporarily – prepared to give up his independence. Not so Tsvetaeva: she always accepted isolation as her destiny. And Emily Dickinson throughout her life as a poet was all but a total recluse.

Her admission: 'Because I see – New Englandly' implies the closest of bonds with her native place, Amherst, Massachusetts, and with the still powerful culture prevailing there. 'The Amherst heart', she once said, 'is plain and whole and permanent and warm.' Since she was always precise in

53

her definitions, we may take this as more than a sentimental tribute. Emily Dickinson appreciated Amherst rather as George Eliot (much favoured by her) did the community into which she had been born, admiring the moral fibre yet critical of the prejudices that sustained it. Emily did not seek to participate in the life of Amherst, keenly though she listened to local news. There had been a time, she told one of her few literary friends, T.W.Higginson, when 'my lexicon was my only companion'. This lexicon, Noah Webster's *American Dictionary of the English Language,* gave her, in counterpoise to Shakespeare, a clear insight into the nature of specifically American speech.

A community shows its character above all through the language it uses. In our time artefacts and buildings, clothes and popular music all tend to be similar throughout the world. But language is still not so easily subordinated to the mass culture that increasingly we have to share. It can be flooded with cosmopolitan terms, and the jargon of the mediocre journalist everywhere conforms to the same pattern, even political vocabulary making little more than a surface variation. But the language of experience still works at a deeper level. To become expressive for the individual it must draw upon a local idiom, upon ways of speech, tones and discriminations which have been evolved by the community. An English reader will recognise that Emily Dickinson, steeped though her mind was in the Bible, Shakespeare and Sir Thomas Browne, yet takes her characteristic note from the New England voices of the neighbourhood:

> You are sure there's such a person
> As 'a Father' in the sky –

54

So if I get lost − there − ever
Or do what the nurse calls 'die' −
I shan't walk the 'Jasper' barefoot −
Ransomed folks won't laugh at me?
Maybe 'Eden' a'n't so lonesome
As New England used to be!

Or where the feeling is more exposed:

I got so I could hear his name
Without − tremendous gain −
That stop-sensation on my soul
And thunder in the room.

I got so I could walk across
That angle in the floor,
Where he turned so, and I turned − how −
And all our sinew tore.

I got so I could stir the box
In which his letters grew
Without that forcing, in my breath −
As staples driven through [. . .]

The quiet tone, the homeliness of the images, the violence −
all this shows what it is to see, and to speak, 'New Englandly'.

It was a deliberate choice that had confined Emily Dickinson to her room, but whether she wanted it or not, she was imprisoned in the New England culture of her time. On this Allen Tate, a southerner, has written with the clairvoyance sometimes achieved by an outsider who is at once repelled and attracted by what he finds both familiar and strange. Tate saw her as coming on the scene at a turning-point in

New England history. The intense moralism of its culture was soon to decline into the concern with civilised manners that Henry James explored, or, as Tate identifies the stage then reached – 'A whole world-scheme, a complete cosmic background, has shrunk to the dimensions of the individual conscience.'

Marina Tsvetaeva, a wife and the mother of three children, one of whom died of famine, was out in the world, and had no protection from its cruelties. She spent long years of adversity in the emigration (Berlin, Czechoslovakia, finally Paris) before following her husband back to the Soviet Union and eventual suicide. Tsvetaeva wrote of herself, a White sympathiser in the revolutionary Moscow of 1919:

> I have many souls. But my principal soul is German. In me there are many rivers, but my principal river is the Rhine.

Her mother, half Baltic German, half Polish, brought her up to love German poetry and music. Marina called Germany 'my passion, my native land, cradle of my soul!' Fifteen years later, in the poem 'Homesickness' she protested that the 'milky call' of her native tongue did not allure her, since those she met would misunderstand whatever language she spoke. Yet in spite of these protestations Tsvetaeva had an almost uncanny feeling for what one poem of hers named 'the pliancy of the Russian tongue'. Joseph Brodsky has emphasised her dependence on it. He quotes the opening lines of another poem:

> The poet takes his speech from far away.
> By his speech the poet is taken far.

He states that, with the exception of one peasant writer in

her time, Tsvetaeva among all its greatest Russian poets 'stands the nearest to folklore' and especially to the folk lament (*prichitanie*). In her poetry and her prose she plays continually with the language; but the play is intent and serious, as the poet learns to define and explore her identity under its guidance.

Brodsky cites 'a poem by her beloved Rilke, later translated by the Pasternak she loved', in which the evening star is compared with the light in the window of 'the last house at the end of the village'. Like this star, he says, which 'only magnifies the idea the parishioners have of their parish bounds', so Tsvetaeva's poetry, highly individual as it is in Russian literature, reveals that literature's full dimension. In no society could she feel at home: opposition came to her instinctively. Her dilemma was very plain. 'There', she said, meaning in the Soviet Union, 'they would not print me — and have read me; here [in France] they print and don't read me.' She maintained: 'Every poet is essentially an émigré, even in Russia.' Or, more shockingly, as her *Poem of the End* expresses it,

> In this most Christian of worlds
> The poets are Yids.

We have glanced at two extreme cases of the isolated poet. Each was, nevertheless, a philologist, a daughter of her language as only a poet can be. In the case of Emily Dickinson, the community from which she had withdrawn stayed actively present to her mind, especially in its manner of speaking. Tsvetaeva, in spite of her separateness, had that instinctive affinity with the unlettered Russian people which

Brodsky has noted as a closeness to folklore. What though of the poet who needs to discover a community to which he can belong only by gaining for himself a place in tradition? I should like to consider Eliot and Cavafy, who have been searchingly compared by Seferis from the view-point of one more fortunate than either in the tradition he found available to him.

Eliot's opposite in American poetry and his consistent critic was William Carlos Williams, who rejected Europe, where his friend Pound and later Eliot had gone, out of loyalty to his birthplace, Rutherford, New Jersey. For Williams it was the local that signified: as Lawrence, reviewing his book *In The American Grain,* succinctly put it: 'All creative art must rise out of a specific soil and flicker with a spirit of place.' Eliot carefully laid aside his Americanness to become a European. His allegiance was not to the American soil (even though memories of the Maine coast or the Mississippi, of 'the bent golden-rod and the lost sea smell', surface in his poetry under pressure of feeling). He chose rather 'the mind of Europe' and the tradition which, developing over centuries and millennia, ideally should penetrate it. The Europeans were willing to accept him as one of their poets, even as the most influential of the time; and he became no less authentically a spokesman for the civilisation of Western Europe than, say, Paul Valéry. Williams too achieved what he had aimed at, on the evidence of Robert Lowell who said: 'It's as if no poet except Williams had really seen America or heard its language.'

Eliot remains in the final reckoning an American, regardless of his alignment. The persona was magisterially

European, the voice neutrally correct in its English tones. But the temper of his mind, the voice behind his voice, the exacting conscience, the dryness and asperity, derived from New England, even though he grew up in the Middle West. The dislike he originally felt for Goethe is treated as one sign of 'Puritan prejudices' by a European critic not sharing them, Mario Praz. Eliot's decision to naturalise as an Englishman could be justified by feelings of piety towards a Somerset village, East Coker, from which his ancestors had departed for America. Emotionally it made sense; whether it was right for his poetry time alone could show. The act of naturalisation pertains to the civil sphere; it has to do with a poet's domicile and political allegiance. These will of course make their imprint on his writing. But no one can become an equal participant in another literature, even when its language is the same, and acquire for himself the sense of wholly belonging there.

The poet according to Eliot's prescription must be impersonal. He believed that 'the progress of an artist is a continual self-sacrifice, a continual extinction of personality'. This is related to his belief that the emotions of an experience in life should not be confused with the feelings realised in an eventual poem, in which what was once undergone has been transmuted. Eliot's ideal of impersonality is founded on the desire to escape from private miseries and shames that the public has no business to scrutinise. We should discriminate, I suggest, between two conceptions of impersonality. One – which Eliot here defines but which in his greatest poetry he transcended – is purely negative, an 'extinction of personality'. But there exists also a positive form, in which the writer does not extinguish what is personal but carries it over to the common hearth. In that way the sense of community can be as strong as Akhmatova's when she spoke for the hundred millions of her people, having recognised the universality of a private grief.

Eliot would not have challenged the rhetorical question put by Yeats at the beginning of this century: 'Does not the greatest poetry always require a people to listen to it?' By a people Yeats meant 'a community bound together by imaginative possessions'. Eliot had little hope of finding such a community in the Western world of his time. The audience he tried to reach through his plays, he was well aware, did not trust poetry. Nor did he trust it enough, when he came to write *The Cocktail Party*. The dramatist using verse, he said, confronts 'an unknown and unprepared audience'. The poet, he remarked in *The Use of Poetry and the Use of Criticism*, 'naturally prefers to write for as large and miscellaneous an audience as possible', adding that 'it is the half-educated and ill-educated, rather than the uneducated, who stand in his way'. 'I myself', he admitted, 'should like an audience which could neither read nor write.' The 'people' whom Yeats had in mind as audience for the 'greatest poetry' would be like those he had known in Galway, where legend still flourished, and where, ninety years before, 'Raftery, the wandering country poet', had made the rounds, 'chanting fine verses, and playing badly on his fiddle.' Yeats understood well that 'the perfected minds' which 'express the people' should they be left on their own are a little pool that will soon dry up. A people alone is a great river, and that is why I am persuaded that where a people has died, a nation is about to die.

A similar fear was voiced by Eliot in 1923 when he wrote on the death of the music-hall artist Marie Lloyd. It marked for him 'a significant moment in English history'. The people valued her because 'she embodied the virtues which they most respected in private life'. He called her 'the expressive figure of the lower classes'; and it seemed to him no other class had such an idol, certainly not the 'middle classes' whom he regarded as 'morally corrupt'. With Marie Lloyd there would disappear 'that collaboration of the audience with the artist which is necessary in all art and most obviously in dramatic art'.

Yeats had to abandon his hope that the poetic drama might become 'the art of the people', accepting instead a much more limited audience: 'In the studio and in the drawing-room we can found a true theatre of beauty.' But the studio and the drawing-room return the poet virtually to his isolation. They are little pools that may soon dry up if unable to draw from the springs of a living tradition expressed in a language the people understand. The image of drought – 'if there were the sound of water only' – which Eliot made distinctively his own, acknowledges the plight of modern civilisation, hence the wide resonance it achieved. The poets can now foresee the 'great river' itself, which fertilised the imagination of their predecessors, sinking into the sands. That would bring the deadly boredom of which Eliot warned in his essay on Marie Lloyd, when a collaborative art is replaced by meaningless entertainment.

Seferis believed that Eliot and Cavafy had in common with Flaubert a tone of senility. This was the tone adopted by Cavafy before his fortieth year, by Flaubert 'from a small boy', and by Eliot in 'Prufrock' and 'Gerontion'. All three, he noted, had the historical sense, and the weight of years they carried was the burden of the world they lived in. Moreover, all three wrote with difficulty ('the intolerable wrestle/With words and meanings'). Cavafy, it should be added, was here most at a disadvantage. Seferis could think of no other poet compelled to work in such isolation, and Cavafy's earliest poems offer no sign of a gift for language. Indeed, it seemed to Seferis that the language actually hindered him.

By chance Seferis got to know Cavafy's poems intimately at a time of national and personal crisis. On being evacuated from Crete in 1941 with the Greek government, he soon found himself in Alexandria, the city where Cavafy had lived all his life and where he died only eight years before. It was on arriving at Port Said, to be confronted with the dead level of the landscape, that Seferis felt he now understood Cavafy's poetry: 'prosaic like the boundless plain in front of us'. The Greek sensibility had been formed by the mountains and the sea; Seferis felt himself to be a man whom the sea had bred. But Cavafy was a deeply erudite gentleman, living 'in a half-lit library with expensive carpets', and one would want to take him out for a breath of sea air. However, it was Cavafy's verse that Seferis principally studied when undergoing exile with his government in South Africa.

Cavafy stood apart from other Greek poets of his day because he belonged to a different Hellenic world. His ancestors had been Phanariots, Greeks who occupied high positions in the Ottoman empire, and looked down upon the demotic idiom as barbarous and unserviceable for literature. Cavafy himself, as Seferis comments, was oppressed not by the want of a tradition, which troubled the new poets, but by its overpowering presence. He claimed to be a member of the Hellenic race rather than a Greek citizen (which of course as an Egyptian subject he was not). The home territory of his imagination lay in Asia Minor, among the ancient Greek cities like Antioch and Ephesus, and in his own Alexandria. 'I am an historical poet', he professed – one who lived in a present time only to be understood through the history of his race. He was the spiritual contemporary of Plutarch (upon whom he drew freely) and of Simonides, whose brevity and fatalism were also his. And he consorted with fictitious characters, the poets and orators of Hellenistic cities and obscure kingdoms, through all of which he realised himself. 'Cavafy's genius', it has been observed by Montale, 'lay in the recognition that the Hellene of that time corresponded to *homo europaeus* today.'

The language he devised for his own needs is described by Seferis as Cavafy's special demotic. It came both from his heritage and his environment, the Greek colony in Alexandria. Seferis has called him an eavesdropper noting the idiom of 'the common people or petits bourgeois of the café or the stock exchange'. He redeemed its ungainliness by three virtues – accuracy, agility, and mastery of moral apothegm. These qualities, no less than his profound historical sense, have appealed strongly to foreign poets who are not concerned with his language in the way that Seferis had to be. Zbigniew Herbert and Joseph Brodsky are only two of those whose debt to Cavafy is evident. Milosz, hoping for a renewal that can be gained through possession of the past, turns to him as a poet for the second half of this century. He claims that 'Cavafy is particularly understandable for a Polish poet', since the last two centuries have brought it about that 'the true home of the Polish poet is history'. It may well become the refuge of poets everywhere, since the past can reveal to them a vanished community. However, community in the fullest sense means a joining of past, present and future. In Cavafy's case the future could only be secured by the preservation of that other Greek language, which was not available to him, and has been described by Seferis as 'alive, robust, obstinate and gracious'. This language, in its demotic form, has kept an essential identity over three thousand years, and it remains flexible and inventive.

Community, as the poets have idealised it, is founded on place. That was the conviction of Wordsworth and Hardy in our own literature. Both, it happens, were seekers of solitude, not warm-blooded men; but equally strong for them (perhaps on that very account) was the pull of community. Always it was the common that Wordsworth most appreciated. He responded deeply in Newton to

> a mind forever
> Voyaging through strange seas of Thought, alone.

This was a power he revered in his own imagination. But Wordsworth also wrote that the poet in due course would have to welcome science 'as a dear and genuine inmate of the household of man'. In his poem 'The Brothers' the landscape of the fells is an open book from which the inhabitants may read their chronicle. The Priest says:

> We have no need of names and epitaphs;
> We talk about the dead by our firesides.

His 'poems on the Naming of Places' record little domestic incidents within his own family associated with each. The sense of belonging to a settled place has always been strongly felt by poets. When Dante encounters his crusading ancestor Cacciaguida in paradise he hears from him a celebration of Florence as it had been 'within the ancient ring' of its walls, austere and simple. The greatest good fortune of those Florentine women in Cacciaguida's day was that each could be certain of her burial place. No wonder, then, that Hardy in his essay of 1883, 'The Dorsetshire Labourer', should have grieved over the vagrancy which had been forced upon the agricultural worker, with grave consequences. The bonds of a community had been loosened. He recognised that the new nomads had 'lost touch with their environment, and that sense of long local participancy which is one of the pleasures of age'.

What Hardy noted a hundred years ago was a process that has accelerated powerfully, and not only in the Western world – a steady evacuation of the countryside and the consequent overburdening of cities. In the third world it has been particularly disastrous, as shanty towns spread ever more uncontrollably their squalor and wreckage round urban centres. And in human terms we are seeing the spread of a desert with something like moral famine as the result. Those who had once been individuals with a recognised place in society, however oppressive their conditions, have become what Pope once, in a quite different context, referred to as 'nameless names'.

Perhaps the cruellest effect of this desolation when the masses are driven from the land is that it destroys the future. There can be no future without a shared past, except one of boredom, aimlessness and despair. In the nineteenth century that condition afflicted the 'superfluous men' of Russian society, the Byronic poseurs throughout Europe, the dandies like Baudelaire, and those who felt Flaubert's disgust for the bourgeoisie and the leaden routine of Yonville l'Abbaye (significantly 'named after an ancient Capuchin abbey the ruins of which are no longer extant'). Flaubert had no hope of the common people either. They were sunk in stupefying labour, like the uncomprehending Catherine Leroux who receives her medal for long service at the agricultural show in *Madame Bovary*. Yet in more backward countries it remained an article of faith among many writers that there was such a thing as national genius, finding expression in the language of the simple and uneducated. Juan de Mairena, the 'apocryphal professor' invented by Antonio Machado, is made to say: 'In our literature almost everything that is not folklore is pedantry.' By 'folklore', we are told, he meant 'what the people think and feel [. . .] as they express and shape this in the language which they more than anyone contributed to form.' Gogol greatly admired the aptness and vigour of Russian popular speech, and a century later Andrey Sinyavsky found it still flourishing in the Gulag. What is it that sustains such vitality, whether in Russia or Spain or Greece?

Machado's great-uncle had been a collector of traditional *romances* or folk ballads, and Machado himself wanted to write his own *romances* emanating, he said,

not from heroic deeds, but from the people that composed them and the land where they were sung; my *romances* regard what is elemental in man, the countryside of Castile, and the First Book of Moses, called Genesis.

So long as the popular imagination could draw on the memory of legend and folk tale, and dramatise life in terms of the Old Testament, there would continue to be a creative community at the base of national literature. The position is admirably put by Seferis: 'What is the language of a country? The living language that the people speak, as it is shaped by its best writers.' He could say that 'from the era of Saint Paul' to Solomos in the early nineteenth century the Greek people 'in conditions that would easily have rendered any other people speechless, had preserved their language in order to hand it on to the educated when Greece had been set free.' In the light of this statement it is possible to appreciate what he meant by saying that 'quite credibly to be illiterate helps rather than hinders the understanding of poetry.'

I do not believe that this view of an intimate bond between popular culture and living poetry is simply romantic, even though it originated in the romantic period. A poet to be sure of his function needs to know the community for which he speaks, to hear its language around him, altering subtly as the conditions of life alter. As a general rule – broken by Tsvetaeva – he or she must not be separated

67

from the native land of this language, the setting whence it has derived symbols and analogies, an atmosphere, a sense of relations or a geography of the mind. We have seen how the imaginative life of the masses can be eroded, so that a central support of poetry is taken away. But a worse alienation, with more drastic consequences because they seem irreversible, may occur in exile; and exile has become in parts of Europe very nearly the common fate of all independent writers.

Dante was their great predecessor, giving the example of his integrity and of eloquent witness to the condition. But in one important sense exile was easier for him than for a modern poet, and even positively beneficial. The experience opened his eyes to larger issues. It made him an Italian patriot, though remaining a Florentine unable to forget the city and her rejection of him. And it conferred an authority which raised him above local politics. The difference in Dante's situation from that of a writer today was that he had not been exiled from his native language. His wanderings throughout northern Italy never took him to places where Tuscan could not be understood, and it was in large measure due to him that the Tuscan dialect became the most honoured form of the vernacular. His exile did not require him to go through the process of naturalisation, as Eliot and Auden chose to, while retaining their sense of having once been part of another community, more distinct in its complexion from the new one than were the sovereign Italian cities from one another in Dante's time.

The European literature longest inured to exile is that of Poland. Vladislav Khodasevich, half Polish himself, and a leading poet in the first wave of Russian emigration in the

post-revolutionary era, has noted that the golden age of
Polish poetry, with Mickiewicz at its head, 'coincides with
the years of national catastrophe'. He admired its 'profound
inward health' and 'creative memory of the motherland'.
Czeslaw Milosz describes Polish poetry as becoming 'a home
for incorrigible hope, immune to historical disasters'. This
was exemplified in its masterpiece, Mickiewicz's poem *Pan
Tadeusz*, which celebrates the Lithuanian countryside of his
childhood. Khodasevich, hearing often its first lines read to
him by his mother, says that he knew 'it was something in-
extricably bound to prayer and to Poland'.

The peculiar circumstances of Polish history – the fact
that for more than a century their native land had disap-
peared from the map, to be absorbed into Russia, Austria and
Prussia – did not prevent Polish poets from forming a community of hope in the resurrection of Poland. Rather it made
this resource all the more necessary. Even so, Mickiewicz
himself after not many years in exile gave up poetry for lec-
turing and politics. No doubt the Polish example encouraged
Khodasevich to assert that 'the nationality of literature is
formed by its language and spirit, and not by territory [. . .]
nor by a way of life'.

That hope proved fallacious. Nothing like a national
literature – a firmly based alternative to Soviet literature –
developed between the wars in the scattered émigré com-
munities. The reason for this is clear from the bitter experience of Khodasevich himself. He expressed in a more
desperate form the dilemma that Tsvetaeva recognised: '*Here*
I cannot, cannot, I cannot live and write, *there* I cannot, cannot live and write.' Khodasevich was desperately conscious

that *here* and *there*, the emigration and the millions in
Russia, were separated by an unbridgeable gulf. Russian
literature had broken in two, and what survived of it in
Western Europe was dying for want of a future. He could
see that the emigration showed no concern for the younger
poets who had grown up abroad. This was a community in
total decline, sharing in that 'European night' which gave
the title to his last meagre collection of verse.

Thirty years ago, in his preface to *The Captive Mind*,
Milosz wrote: 'My mother tongue, work in my mother
tongue, is for me the most important thing in life.' Every
poet enduring exile would echo this. But the mother
tongue, under those conditions, is in a state of siege.
Vladimir Nabokov, on first arriving in Cambridge as an
undergraduate at Trinity, chanced to find in the market a
copy of the richest of all Russian lexicons, Dahl's *Explanatory Dictionary of the Living Russian Tongue*. From its
four volumes he studied a daily stint to refresh his feeling
for the language. For a decade and more he wrote poems
and prose fiction in 'the living Russian tongue'. Later, in
America, he moved across to English, even translating
many of his Russian works. *Lolita* was composed in
English. The postscript to the Russian edition, which
Nabokov had himself translated, tells 'a tale of disenchant-
ment'. For years he had been assuring the American reader
that Russian was a superior language to English (the point
however may be contested). But when Nabokov came at last
to open the gates where that 'marvellous Russian language'
should have been flowering in all its springtime glory, he
was to find 'nothing there but charred stumps and an

autumnal prospect without hope'. The key in his hand had turned into a lock-pick.

Is there however more hope in that other form of exile which has been known since early Soviet days as 'internal emigration'? The charge of belonging to this category was levelled at various times against Akhmatova, Mandelstam and Pasternak. Their offence, which had estranged them from the community, lay in obstinately adhering to a view of poetry and a moral scheme which could have no place in the new order. Clearly the situation in Soviet Russia was extreme, but it has since been repeated in other countries where totalitarian rule, political or religious, prevails. In that situation the poet is severed from the community not by geographical but spiritual distance. The émigré finds it hard not to compromise with the foreign society that tolerates him. But the opposition poet at home will not be tolerated at all unless he compromises by more than adjusting a way of life. He has to shuffle in matters of belief, to retreat from his most profound convictions. Ideology in whatever shape, when it is imposed by a ruling caste, brings danger to poetry. Even Dante, whose acceptance of Christian belief was whole-hearted, did not escape imputations of heresy on certain points of doctrine. Among the Bolsheviks in power, one of those more sympathetic to the poet's need for independence was Trotsky. But Trotsky made it absolutely clear in his treatise of 1924, *Literature and Revolution,* that 'in general, the place of art is in the rear of the historical advance'. Whenever the artist would appear to have rivalled the politician in foresight, according to Trotsky this is not really so. The Marxist had been guided in his steps by scientific reasoning;

the poet, one has to assume, by no more than a muddled response to seismic changes in society. 'We stepped into the Revolution', Trotsky could claim, 'while Futurism fell into it.'

The question arises whether in our own Western democracies the poet will not gradually be driven into this kind of exile, an internal emigration. Literature is already becoming industrialised to crisis point. This shows in the proliferation of prizes and the malign publicity which surrounds their award. A book, if it is to bring more than a very moderate return to its author, now has to be publicised, and he must consent to put himself in the hands of the skilled promoters. There have been times when literary critics became too powerful, particularly when they imposed ideological demands, even if not backed by the state, as the Russian populists did in the nineteenth century, with an unfortunate legacy for the twentieth. Today in the West, it is the communicators, the television front men, the ubiquitous personalities, who threaten to corrupt the proper audience for art. We cannot have the pollster or the trend-spotter supreme in the arbitration of literary merit.

To compare the situation of a poet in our society today with that of Akhmatova or Mandelstam in the Soviet Union half a century ago is, of course, unrealistic. But the warning signs must not be neglected. Nobody can foresee the state of the free world by the end of this century. And this makes it more imperative to consider the case of Mandelstam in particular, since he was probably the greatest poet of his age to be condemned to internal emigration, and the strongest in meeting the challenge. His three years of exile in Voronezh isolated him from almost everyone apart from occasional visitors, though he did have the support of his wife. Some of the poems written at this time express the utmost desolation:

> I look frost in the face, alone:
> It goes nowhere, I came from nowhere [. . .]

Or he looks at the houses barred against the freezing weather,

> crying
> To some frozen wooden box:
> 'A reader! an adviser! a doctor!
> On the jagged stairway to have some talk!'

Yet contrary to all expectation many of the poems rejoice in life and are hopeful. It is as though Mandelstam had recognised the truth which Montale found when he said that Kafka in his solitude had been able to communicate best of all. Mandelstam believed with full justification that his poetry no longer worked against the main stream of Russian literature but had now merged with it. In his enforced separation from the people, appealing vainly to closed doors for a few words of conversation, he was still assured that his poetry would eventually reach them. This was certain because he had kept faith with his own conscience, and so could trust in the language to assert the truth of his and the people's situation.

CHAPTER 4

THE INTERNATIONAL CODE OF POETRY

Among an impressive array of Russian words for nonsense there is a term that may be translated as 'gibberish', *volapyuk*. This is derived from an over-elaborate and ill-starred predecessor of Esperanto called Volapük. There may still just conceivably be old persons who exchange international greetings in the language. But I doubt whether anybody has tried to compose poetry in Volapük; the result in any case would not have been successful. 'Genuine poetry', Eliot believed, 'can communicate before it is understood.' Volapük presumably was intelligible to its users, but it did not communicate in the full sense. On the other hand Lewis Carroll's 'Jabberwocky', like other good nonsense verse, communicates rather well. A recent Moscow anthology of English poetry in Russian translation included two enterprising attempts, and a note describes the original as 'one of the best examples of English poetic nonsense'.

The German priest who devised Volapük a little over a hundred years ago set about the task from the wrong starting-point. But the quest for an international language, to be acquired easily, has ended with a similar deficiency; it is inorganic, a vehicle cannibalised by its inventor. There has been much interest in the idea of a common language already there waiting to be revealed. One may think of a critic much admired today, Walter Benjamin. In his essay 'The Task of the Translator' (1915–16) he assumed the 'central kinship of languages', and he valued translation because in it 'the great motif of integrating many tongues into one true language is at work'. A translation should 'incorporate the original's mode of signification', so that it and the original become 'recognisable as fragments of a greater language, just as fragments are part of a vessel'.

This is clearly a mystical view. It can be matched by the endeavour of Velimir Khlebnikov a few years before. The philologist Roman Jakobson esteemed him above all contemporary Russian poets because Khlebnikov had elaborated his own system of phonemes in Russian speech. He wrote a famous poem about words beginning with the letter *l*, all of which he believed to indicate 'a gravitational force proceeding on a certain axis and spreading over a surface horizontal to that axis.' This explanation he gave in a prose piece citing a mass of examples, among them *lyzha*, a ski, *lodka*, a boat, *ladon'*, the palm of a hand, *luzha*, the puddle made by falling raindrops. The system, needless to say, becomes strained and fantastic, but Khlebnikov seriously expected it to show him the foundations of a universal language. The scientific aspect I had better leave to the more expert or the more credulous. His effect upon Russian poetry was profound. The new relationship it explored between sound and sense led, as Jakobson's brilliant associate Yury Tynyanov remarked, to the renewal of long forgotten ties of kinship between words and the suggestion of unsuspected ones; and through the exposure of these affinities it gave poetry a binding force which the same critic elsewhere reckoned to be stronger than logic itself. Tynyanov made this latter comment on the poetic procedure of Pasternak, which earlier had much in common with Khlebnikov's, as did Mayakovsky's. An apt image for Khlebnikov was found by Mandelstam who compared him in his dealings with words to a mole 'that dug in the earth tunnels into the future for the entire century'.

Marina Tsvetaeva was so fearlessly original that she could take her own route to the same discoveries. No other poet either in Russian or Western literature of the time, I suspect, lived so intensely by what Eliot called the 'auditory imagination'. This he defined as

the feeling for syllable and rhythm, penetrating far below the conscious levels of thought and feeling, invigorating every word; sinking to the most primitive and forgotten, returning to the origin and bringing something back, seeking the beginning and the end.

Joseph Brodsky, who has written more sensitively about her work than any other critic I know, remarks of her prose what is no less true of her poetry. Because Tsvetaeva, he says, was 'taken extraordinarily far by language, she proves to have been the most interesting thinker of her time'. As he explains elsewhere, 'A poet is one for whom each word is not the end but the beginning of thought'; and Tsvetaeva's way with words is to conduct a perpetual and daring exploration, recovering and enlarging the sense, 'returning to the origin and bringing something back'. It is a great advantage for Russian poets that their art is still primarily an oral medium.

Mandelstam, for instance, was always conscious of the lips stirring, the whole body involved in the making of verse. His apprehension of the Italian language was strikingly physical, and in this connection he remarked:

The inner image of the verse is inseparable from countless changes of expression, flitting across the face of the narrator as he speaks in his excitement.

Tsvetaeva herself achieved exactly what she admired in the memoirs of Prince Volkonsky:

the living and singing Russian idiom, as it yet sings in the villages and in the retentive hearts of the poets.

There is nothing deliberately archaic in this, she maintained, no careful preservation of relics in a museum. Her practice confirms what Eliot had further said of the auditory imagination: it 'fuses the most ancient and the most civilised mentality'.

When poetry returns to the origins, to the primitive and enduring, it reaches what lies far below consciousness of its own time and place. Tsvetaeva explains in an essay of capital significance, 'The Poet and Time':

The legend on one of today's boundary posts – *In the future there will be no frontiers* – is already realised in art, has been so from the beginning.

Mandelstam likewise had written before her of the breaking down by poetry of national frontiers, when 'the elemental in one language calls to another over the heads of space and time'. This view of 'a fraternal alliance' between the languages was shared by poets of the Acmeist school to which Mandelstam and Akhmatova at first belonged, and it is, I would say, eminently Russian.

Anyone surveying European poetry – let us suppose an intelligent enquirer from another part of the world today, or one of our own descendants in a future when Europe has long been merged in a global culture – cannot fail to note how manifestly it all holds together, and for how many centuries this has been so. He is faced by a single literature using a diversity of tongues, and these latter belong for the most part to three main groupings that had a common origin. From one age to another he will see everywhere at work the same process of change and renewal, and a constant mutual awareness between the participants in an all-embracing tradition. Mandelstam liked to think of poetry as 'a plough, turning up time in such a way that time's deep layers, its black earth, show on the surface.'

What he said is in accord with Eliot's well-known perception that often 'the most individual parts' of a poet's work 'may be those in which the dead poets, his ancestors, assert their immortality most vigorously'. Thus Mandelstam could discover in Verlaine a new Villon, and searching for a modern poet akin to Dante, after first trying Baudelaire and Verlaine, settled upon Rimbaud, whom Dante had anticipated as 'a subverter of sense' making images fluid and dynamic. Here he seizes upon a very important truth – not only that the poetic mind perceives reality through its own ambient atmosphere of the poetry that already exists, but also that from this life-giving atmosphere it draws the breath of its being.

There still remains one difficulty we must not overlook. The poets themselves can certainly divine and capture something essential in foreign poetry. A familiar but

nonetheless startling example is that of Pound's dealing with
the Anglo-Saxon poem 'The Seafarer':

> May I for my own self song's truth reckon,
> Journey's jargon, how I in harsh days
> Hardship endured oft.
> Bitter breast-cares have I abided,
> Known on my keel many a care's hold,
> And dire sea-surge, and there I often spent
> Narrow nightwatch nigh the ship's head
> While she tossed close to cliffs.

A chorus of scholars, rightly mistrusting Pound's knowledge
of foreign tongues, for he was a very haphazard linguist, have
protested that his versions in general are loaded with inac-
curacies and freedoms. And yet the first line speaks for Pound
as well as for the seafarer. He has for his own self reckoned
'song's truth'. The peculiar resonance of the original comes
through, in a manner that no modern translator of Old
English verse had been able to convey, if indeed before
Pound fully to perceive, unless it were Tennyson, though his
rendering of 'The Battle of Brunanburh' is much inferior to
Pound's poem. In fact, Pound has achieved what Pasternak is
said to have done when translating the verse of a Georgian
poet, Titsian Tabidze: he sensed what Tabidze himself, re-
joicing in the translations, called the 'inner melody' of the
poems. In the same way, Mandelstam's elegy which he entitled 'Tristia', thereby proclaiming its affiliation to Ovid's
poems from exile, attains a genuine Latin ring, as Tynyanov
observes, by introducing the entirely foreign word *vigilia*,
which changes the chemistry of the whole stanza. I make bold
to say further that Mandelstam's renderings from the *Chan-*

son de Roland and *La Vie de Saint Alexis* catch perfectly the rather stiff nobility of Old French verse.

Yet, if poetry does have what I claimed in the title of this lecture, an international code, we must assume that not only the poets themselves but intelligent readers (or auditors) of poetry can decipher it too. Eliot stated his proposition that 'genuine poetry can communicate before it is understood' in an essay introducing Dante to a public consisting not of poets alone, and he takes it for granted that the 'direct shock of poetic intensity' coming across to him from certain passages will affect any perceptive reader. If he is right, can those of us who are not poets hope that eventually communication for us will be elevated to understanding?

Eliot observed elsewhere that 'feeling and emotion are particular, whereas thought is general. It is easier to think in a foreign language than it is to feel in it. Therefore no art is more stubbornly national than poetry.' He goes on to say that 'a feeling or emotion expressed in a different language is not the same feeling or emotion'. There is undeniably in every poem, however simple it may appear, a burden of connotation. It evokes – and this is heightened by the rhythm of the poem, by subtleties of tone, and pauses and accelerations, which the foreigner may not sufficiently heed – a response in the memory of its own people, for them immediate, but not quickened in the same way for us. Consider the intonations of Robert Frost, and how much for all their apparent flatness they signify. As Frost warned: 'Remember the sentence sound often says more than the words. It may even as in irony convey a meaning opposite to the words.' The exact emphasis of a line by Frost only perhaps an American (or

80

possibly even a native of New Hampshire) can be depended upon to take.

The single voice, then, is nothing without its implication of a community, and, as we have seen, the community falls apart, loses its meaning, without the exercise of memory through language perpetually renewed to bind together its present, past and future. This we become most keenly aware of when confronting a foreign language, in which some of the resonances will be clear, while some are no more than half apprehended. An alert foreigner may have the sense of doors ajar and yet refusing to open at his touch. However, the faculty of listening to poetry in our own language ought to save us from misreading the signs. It may seem ominous that Ossian, or the early Byron, or total Swinburne have at various times been extravagantly admired overseas. Pasternak strangely enough does not appear to have noted the difference in quality between Keats and Swinburne. We must conclude that he was temporarily off his guard: he did not listen attentively, any more than other foreign (and home) admirers of these poets. Their approach to all three was, I suggest, too loosely romantic — that is to say, yielding to the rather crude rhythms, and too easily satisfied with the visual impression the poets evoke, the pictorial flow.

For Eliot, of course, Dante's '*visual* imagination' — 'visual', it is explained, 'in the sense that he lived in an age in which men still saw visions' — accounted to a large degree for this poet's lucidity, together with the nearness of his Italian to medieval Latin, then understood by all educated Europeans. There is undoubtedly a supreme pleasure to be had from such limpid exposition as Dante's. Take, for example, the very first lines of the *Paradiso,* in which he celebrates the presence of light in the celestial regions, a presence that fills the whole canticle:

> La gloria di colui che tutto move
> per l'universo penetra e risplende
> in una parte più e meno altrove.

'The radiance of him who moves all/penetrates the universe and shines out/in one part more and less in another'. Patrick Boyde justly remarks that here 'Dante achieves his own unique blend of precision and sublimity', and the stanza could not be simpler to apprehend. But even here what is crucial to the lines, and also to the entire *Paradiso* – a sense of joy and confidence – is imparted by the 'inner melody'. And that finds expression in the exquisite movement of the lines, which have all the grace of the dancing in a courtly masque. It is no exaggeration to say that the dance of beatitude is sustained to the end of the poem. Unless my ear has deceived me, the movement is briefly checked four lines from the conclusion, when Dante has to confess that here imagination was at a loss:

> All' alta fantasía qui mancò possa.

That unusual stress on the tenth syllable seems to interrupt the dance, but only for an instant. Then triumphantly with the image of a smoothly running wheel it is resumed, and a gentle rotation sets in, as the poet's desire and will are moved by divine love –

> l'amor che move il sole e l'altre stelle.

Dante's meaning was never in doubt, though it is, to borrow an image from Wordsworth, 'carried into the heart' by

82

this dancing effect. No poem was ever so consonant with itself at such unbroken length as *The Divine Comedy*. When you return to the opening of the *Paradiso* after reading its close, Dante's orchestration of feeling is heard with a redoubled delight.

Let us see how the auditory imagination will help in a more difficult instance. Anna Akhmatova had been air-lifted from Leningrad early in the assault on the city; she did not come home from Central Asia until the siege was over. Terrible things had happened in her absence − an inexpressible calamity. Here are some of the grim details, as told by the Greek scholar Olga Freidenberg, first cousin and life-long friend of Pasternak:

December brought a double intensification: of the frosts and of hunger [...] The city lacked fuel [...] People began to swell up with hunger ... Day after day, week after week, no rations were issued [...] In Leningrad that winter there died, so rumour went, 3½ million people [...] [In the new year] there were no trams, there was no lighting, the telephone was cut off. [...] The radio went dead. In that deathly silence, which had gripped even Bolshevik agitation, something terrible was contained. All the surrounding world had fallen away.

I referred to the suffering as inexpressible. But a poet will want to find utterance for it, and Akhmatova wrote a short poem which is now given in bald translation:

> Leningrad's disaster
> With my hands I shall not undo,
> With tears wash away,
> Bury in the earth.
> I shall go a long way round
> Leningrad's disaster.

83

> With no glance, no hint,
> No word, no reproach,
> > I with a bow to the earth
> > In the green field
> > Will remember.

The poem is printed on the page in part for a visual effect, as with some poems by George Herbert. The last three lines are stepped to the right, as though to enact her ritual bowing to the earth in sorow. They lead with a diminuendo to the single word in Russian [*pomyanú*] for 'will remember', on its own like the poet herself before the incomprehensible agony of it all. However, until we have heard the poem, how much of its full experience will be communicated?

The effect is very different when the opening lines are heard in Russian:

> Leningrádskuyu bedú
> Rukámi ne razvedú,
> Slezámi ne smóyu,
> V zémlyu ne zaróyu.

You will have detected a note of intense pain, audible from the opening phrase *Leningrádskuyu bedú*, Leningrad's disaster, the source of the poet's anguish. The poem is entitled *Prichitanie*, keening, and these are the accents of folk lament, to be heard in countless Russian songs, and traditional too is the gesture, described with such dignified movement, of bowing deeply in compassion. We may have only the drift of Akhmatova's sense, and yet those four lines surely communicate what she means – 'far below the conscious levels of thought', as Eliot put it. In the last sentence translation cannot bring out the effect of the personal pronoun I, which introduces each of its first three lines: 'I with no glance, no hint,/I with no word, no reproach,/I with a bow to the earth [...]' This repetition might seem to give undue prominence to the poet herself; it does no such thing. The 'I' impresses rather as a stepping forward from the anonymous ranks on their behalf to 'remember' – the poet's function – by her act of reverence to the afflicted city. Her 'I' is the representative of the people, confirmed in this office by the traditional form of lamentation, and, as the final solitary word emphasises, she also stands for the individual human being in the face of a hideous calamity for which no words of comfort are conceivable.

Eliot cannot be challenged when he says that poetry has 'a unique value for the people of the poet's race and language, which it can have for no other'. Yet it becomes possible for practised readers of poetry to hear in a foreign poem, like this one by Akhmatova, a specific national tone which they too begin to appreciate, and thereby to enlarge their sympathies, even their capacity for feeling. Because our own poetry derives far back in time from a common root, no matter how divergent, say, our alliterative system may be from the native traditions of Russian verse, the emotion in Akhmatova's lament is strongly communicated. The ancestral spirits of a common culture arise from barely perceived depths to work on our feelings too, when we learn to attend. The essential rapport between one nation's poetry and another's, if they are held in a common tradition such as has prevailed in Europe, is stronger than any barriers to communication.

At the beginning of the 1930s Mandelstam was reading

85

Dante, Tasso and Ariosto, with some uneasiness about the beguiling euphony of the last two; and also the German romantics while looking afresh at some of his Russian predecessors. It was then that he wrote his poem 'To the German Language' in which he declares:

> Let us learn seriousness and honour
> In the west from an alien family

– though not of course, as his poem makes clear, a family so alien to himself with his German surname and a father who had brought German books with him to St Petersburg from Riga. The poem was dated only a few months before German seriousness and honour were devastated by Hitler's coming to power, though it is important to note that by all accounts they are prominent again in much poetry from both successor republics in our own period. There is even something of a deliberate German texture to the verse of this poem, since to learn the moral values of a people will require from the poet some assimilation of their characteristic tones into his language. This has happened in our own poetry through the ages and we can all recognise French or Latin or Italian characteristics in English verse when they are met. However, the point at issue just now is a different one. Nobody, I assume, will deny that foreign influences can bear upon poetry, and for the most part they enrich it, although there are even some poets in England today who seem to regard the reading of poetry in other tongues as a kind of self-preening tourism. But a larger body of objectors is likely to raise its voice about an assumption made many times in these lectures.

How can you learn 'seriousness and honour' from poetry, now that sophisticated people − so the argument goes − no longer speak of Victorian values anyway without casting doubt on their moral basis while deploring some of their visible effects? And is it not an exploded Victorian prejudice to see in poetry a means to edification, as when Arnold spoke of its being able to impart 'influences of refining and elevation'? Yet these poets from Russia and Eastern Europe seem to take it for granted that, in Nadezhda Mandelstam's words, poetry constitutes 'the golden treasury in which our values are preserved; it brings people back to life, awakens their consciousness and stirs them to thought.' They never question that the poet alone is responsible for what he says, or that using the text as a mere starting point for a much more interesting exhibition of what can be done with it once the author has been ejected, amounts to a betrayal of literary conscience. Milosz being an East European sees all too clearly the pernicious effect of this procedure. Just as he had quoted Simone Weil on the gross derelictions of Dada and surrealism before the Second World War, so in his Nobel Lecture of 1980 he states unequivocally:

There is, it seems, a hidden link between theories of literature as *écriture*, of speech feeding on itself, and the growth of the totalitarian state.

The very word 'golden treasury' which Max Hayward used to translate *zolotoy fond*, 'gold reserves', is redolent of Palgrave and the 1860s, precisely the decade in which emphasis on the moral purpose of literature was most firmly established by the Russian utilitarian critics, Chernyshev-

sky, Dobrolyubov and Pisarev. When Mrs Mandelstam asked herself 'why all those students who thirst after truth and
righteousness are always so keen on poetry', it is clear that she
had never heard about the disillusionment of Laura Riding.
Well known as poet and theorist of poetry before the Second
World War, she has published no verse since her *Collected
Poems* of 1938. By then she had begun 'to see poetry dif-
ferently, even as a harmful ingredient of our linguistic life'. It
seemed to her that poetry 'veers from the path of natural
linguistic difficulties to follow the line of art'. The objection
is positively Tolstoyan in its distrust of the way in which
poetic method interferes with the delivery of plain truth, and
it leads her to the conclusion that poetry is able 'to clarify
nothing, to change nothing.' Yet Andrey Sinyavsky, in a
famous essay on *samizdat* writing, has told us that 'beside the
cradle' of *samizdat* 'there stood the shades of the greatest
twentieth century poets'.

Our divided world is undergoing on both sides a crisis of
confidence, and this centres upon the use of words, especially
of words by public figures. I doubt whether any generation
has been so much aware of the treachery in language, when it
is trusted too readily. Everywhere people have grown wary of
rhetoric (almost invariably used today as a derogatory term),
and it is not only 'the voices of temptation' attacking 'the
Word in the desert' that put us on guard. The very nature of
language seems to oppress the mind with a burden of in-
herited prejudices and assumptions; it can be inert as well as
sensitive to our human impulses; barbarous in its unexamin-
ed metaphors; constantly exposing the limitations of words
as an instrument of thinking; opaque where it should be

luminous, deceptively clear where there is confusion below
the surface. All these charges are real, and they have to be
answered by the modern poet if he is to feel confidence in his
art. There are those like Tadeusz Różewicz in Poland who
have freely confessed: 'I regard my poems with acute
mistrust', because the words must be taken from 'the great
rubbish dump, the great cemetery' created for his countrymen by the Second World War. Another Polish poet,
Zbigniew Herbert, was asked in an interview: ' "Honour,
loyalty, constancy" – what do these words mean nowadays?
Can they make a poem?' He conceded that 'they belong to a
smashed table of values', adding:

'In our time such concepts may be hinted at, discussed. One can
point out what they mean in a given situation and prove that they
are still binding and important. Great words should be spared. One
must see the inter-relations of words.

It is here that the importance of memory comes into the
argument. We know that in our own country an earlier age
had a much more exact and extensive moral vocabulary than
we use today in our dealings with one another. Put beside the
orderly and efficient ranks at Jane Austen's service, our own
ragged and scanty retinue makes a pitiful showing. We have
that down at heels and exhausted maid of all work, compassion; there is integrity, invoked when anyone is not patently
dishonest; and there is wise counsel, which is found invariably to have been given, unsuspected by most of us, when
a colleague retires. On the debit side, we have lost the distinction between sensuous and sensual, masterly and masterful;
disinterest was so little employed that it needed to be given a

new job; and for anything abhorrent, from ugly wall paper to genocide, there is the all purpose word, obscene. I may exaggerate a little, though in dark moments one forbodes a time when we shall be left with two simple alternatives – obscene and great. Poetry, our best remembrancer, has not forgotten the others, and it can show what Herbert means, I think, by inter-relations, their coming to life in the appropriate context.

We seek from the past more than political understanding, or the meaning of national identity, though the latter is very much bound up with a moral vocabulary we can all share. What can be found in the poetry of earlier generations, and, I must emphasise, in that of other peoples as well as our own, is a safeguard and a promise. There is in genuine poetry a depth of moral awareness, of involuntary truth, and a capacity to set human experience where it can be judged without special pleading or undue harshness. Poetry achieves this by a process of reconciliation and acceptance (not the same thing as capitulation): a reconciliation with the limits of what is possible for human beings, an acceptance of community.

Antonio Machado makes his fictitious preceptor, Juan de Mairena, say on one occasion: 'If we were forced to choose a poet we should choose Shakespeare, that gigantic creator of consciences.' And in parenthesis he adds a question that seems very relevant here: 'Is Shakespeare English or England Shakespearian?'

The delicacy of moral awareness in Shakespeare's poetry has never been more quietly convincing than in the words given to Lear on his knees before Cordelia. This is probably one of the most familiar passages in our literature, but I ask you, with some hesitation, to consider it once again, for it shows how the right inter-relation of words sets the seal upon reconciliation and acceptance as the insights achieved by poetry at its purest:

> Pray, do not mock me:
> I am a very foolish fond old man,
> Fourscore and upward, not an hour more or less;
> And, to deal plainly,
> I fear I am not in my perfect mind.
> Methinks I should know you and know this man;
> Yet I am doubtful; for I am mainly ignorant
> What place this is, and all the skill I have
> Remembers not these garments; nor I know not
> Where I did lodge last night. Do not laugh at me;
> For, as I am a man, I think this lady
> To be my child Cordelia.

Lear cannot remember how he comes to be there, or know for sure who are the people round him. In that respect, memory has deserted this broken old man, and when this happens identity is clouded. But in a more important respect memory can still function, and he is able to interpret the moment to himself and to others almost with the surefooted-ness of a sleepwalker, as familiar expressions come to his lips: 'foolish fond old man', 'to deal plainly', 'not in my perfect mind', 'as I am a man'. They are the phrases known to all, well worn, but suddenly revived here in their full meaning. The movement of Shakespeare's verse, as Lear tries to define the position, is calm and instinctively right. This is the voice of one who for the first time listens to himself, spelling out his situation for it to become clear in the final statement:

91

> For, as I am a man, I think this lady
> To be my child Cordelia.

The stock phrase, 'as I am a man', now has a greatly enhanced meaning, for he understands that the lady before him is his own child. Lear steps back into human society because he is able to perceive his dual relationship with Cordelia. On the one hand he respects her, as — to use an old-fashioned phrase which here may carry more than the social definition it includes — a person of quality. On the other, he finds in a sense he had not morally grasped before, that she is his offspring. Cordelia has been restored to him, now that he has become himself. This, I need hardly point out, briefly foreshadows the pattern of the last plays. In its muted fashion, the music of acceptance sounds here no less triumphantly than it does there:

> I think this lady
> To be my child Cordelia.

Twice at least, towards the end of his life, Matthew Arnold spoke of being able to 'trust the instinct of self-preservation in humanity'. He thought this would show itself by 'keeping Greek as part of our culture', and here unfortunately he was mistaken. On the earlier occasion it had been the 'currency and supremacy' of 'good literature' which he believed this instinct was bound to ensure. There, we must admit, the issue still hangs in the balance. Milosz, with his eye very much on the present time, quotes in the Nobel Lecture his cousin Oscar's opinion, that 'putting the second-rate on the same level as the first-rate' is 'a major sin'. How far, we are bound to ask, is the instinct for self-preservation in humanity alive at this close of an extraordinary millennium? To pose the question still more starkly, does the notion of a self mean today, in Western or Eastern Europe, what Arnold himself must have understood by it?

Again on both sides of Europe the self is under assault, though in different ways, and of course not to the same degree here. Among the Eastern peoples it has been threatened with obliteration of memory, of all record, along with the falsifying or suppression of historical evidences. The hardest thing of all in the Gulag would appear to be retaining a sense of time; as the calendar dissolves, it takes away the sequence of events and also the perception of any purpose. In the West there is a double threat, neither of them perhaps as yet fully understood. The first form is revealed in the erosion of privacy, its willing surrender by those who seek public notice. If you wish to extract intimate secrets from someone, all that need be done is to arrange an interview on television. This eager baring of the self, which strangely evaporates in the process, is no less remarkable than the abject self-incrimination which astonished the world in the first great Moscow show trials of the 1930s, though these could be explained by a refined inquisitorial technique playing on a Dostoevskyan impulse to self-abasement. It is matched by the prerogative claimed for journalists to intrude upon anything in the personal life, however painful. There is a very widespread desire to belittle and debase, to search for corruption everywhere; and few people today wince at the anguish caused in others by malicious anecdote and heavy innuendo. Headlines today are too often interchangeable between newspapers at every level; and they nearly all of them

93

carry the gossip-column as a kind of spinnaker to speed them up in the race for circulation.

These may appear trivial things, but triviality can demoralise almost as successfully as despotism. And Milosz has insisted in his Nobel Lecture that the masses have an 'unavowed need of true values', but that they are without the language to express it.

I hope that by now the crucial importance of poetry has been established. It is indispensable for a number of reasons: for its unrivalled power of recall, which enables it to bring into the present and project into the future truths of feeling attained perhaps three thousand years ago; for its intimacy with every phase of our long developing and changing culture; and above all for its power of self-correction. Writing poetry has always been a demanding process, however spontaneous the flow may sometimes appear to be. It calls for very great discipline in the poet – which helps to explain why the highest poetry is seldom in large supply – and it cannot be forced. Poetry also requires what most of us find very difficult to accept – the willingness, in Keats's words, to endure 'being in uncertainties, mysteries, doubts'. Nineteenth-century optimism, twentieth-century despair – not that either attitude was total at any time – are alike in their unwillingness to face that suspension between extremes, and to live undaunted by contradiction. What Brodsky has admired most of all in Tsvetaeva is her ability to accept the sense of the ambiguous and irresolvable in human life, particularly in the way the present age has been experiencing it, and to use this sense, in all its discomfort and spiritual oppressiveness, as the material for her poetry.

94

We stand today in a position to see more clearly the years that have brought us here than many preceding generations could in their own case. It appears to be always tempting for those with a sense of history to claim that their own age is a turning-point, and never more so than when the calendar imposed by human reckoning approaches an artificial boundary. The close of a millennium presents itself to the imagination as an awesome event. It happens now to fall at a time when rapid change appears to be under way in every department of human life, and the most unexpected challenges are being made to assumptions that had become quite unconscious through immemorial tenure. The old sanctions are melting away; the fabric of societies, conservative or advanced, has come increasingly under strain; irrationality flourishes to an extent that, say, two hundred years ago in Western Europe would have been inconceivable; the difficulties ahead show as more complicated and hard to overcome every year.

When this is so, a real comfort can be derived from the fact that in the twentieth century its greatest poets have not failed in courage or conviction. The harshness of the times has concentrated their minds on far more than a personal predicament. They have been able to prove to themselves and to their audience that the tradition of poetry is indestructible. Through its peculiar concern with the inter-relation of words, it has been able to explore ambiguities so as not to frustrate but to deepen communication. It has kept alive in extremity the individual conscience, the notion of freedom in play, and, more strangely perhaps, the persistence of joy.

Only when one reads, for example, how the friends of

95

Mandelstam and Akhmatova risked their own lives to take custody of a few scraps of verse, is it possible to realise fully what poetry can mean. If the poetic word were to be silenced, despotism and emptiness would rule everywhere. The experience of more than one generation shows it will not be silenced.

REFERENCES

The renderings of quotations in verse are my own.

1. *The function of poetry at the present time*

T. S. Eliot's *The Use of Poetry and the Use of Criticism* was first published in 1933 (paperback edn., London, 1964). His quotations from Norton appear in the Introduction and in the lecture on Matthew Arnold. The latter's essay, 'The Function of Criticism at the Present Time' dates from 1864, and was placed at the head of his *Essays in Criticism* (London, 1865). Czeslaw Milosz' *The Witness of Poetry* was published in 1983 (Cambridge, Mass. and London); his book *The Captive Mind* (English translation, 1953) is available in paperback (London, 1980).

Lawrence writes of the decisive moment 1915–16 in the chapter of *Kangaroo* (1923; paperback edn., London, 1950) entitled 'The Nightmare'. Mayakovsky's prophecy for the year 1916 was made in the second part of his 'tetraptych' poem, *A Cloud in Trousers* [*Oblako v shtanakh*, 1915]. Akhmatova's 'real twentieth century' is presented as ominously near in the third chapter of her 'triptych' *Poem Without a Hero* [*Poema bez geroya*, 1940–62], in a scene that she dates 'Petersburg, 1913', at Christmas-tide. Wilfred Owen wrote of his 'seared conscience' in a letter of June 1917, and in another of August in the same year about Tennyson's ignorance of true misery; both are quoted by Edmund Blunden in the 'Memoir'

97

prefacing his edition of *The Poems of Wilfred Owen* (London, 1931). The assault on Beaumont Hamel that led to its capture took place in November 1916. John Terraine in *The Great War 1914–1918* (London, 1965; paperback edn., 1967) states that 'conditions on the Somme at the end of 1916' were generally agreed by survivors to 'surpass all other sensations of horror'.

Lowell's statement 'no profession seemed wispier' was made in an article on William Carlos Williams in the *Hudson Review* 1961–2, which Charles Tomlinson has included in his Penguin Critical Anthology on Williams (London, 1972). The case of George Oppen is discussed by Jeremy Hooker in 'Seeing the World: The Poetry of George Oppen' which appeared in *PN Review*, 41 (Vol. 11, No. 3). Trilling's essay 'Reality in America' has two sections, the first published in 1940, the second in 1946; it is to be found in his book, *The Liberal Imagination* (London, 1951). Blok's question 'Does democracy need the artist?' was entered in his Notebook (April – June 1917) under the date 14 April. The interview with John Ashbery was published in *The Times*, 23 August 1984.

The poem by Seferis 'The Last Day' [*I Televtaia Mera*] is published in the Greek with an English translation by Edmund Keeley and Philip Sherrard, in the *Collected Poems* (London, 1982). Vittorio Sereni draws attention to it in an essay on the filmmaker Theodoros Angelopoulos, reprinted in *Gli immediati dintorni* (Milan, 1983). Seferis rejects Western European conceptions of the Hellenic, from Dante to Hölderlin, in his 'Dialogue on Poetry' [*Dialogos pano stin poisi*, 1938], collected in his *Essays* (*Dokimes, Tomos A'*, Athens, 1981). 'Stratis Thalassinos among the Agapanthi' [*O Stratis Thalassinos anamesa stous agapanthous*, 1942] is also to be found in the *Collected Poems*; it belongs to *Logbook II*. Seferis's tribute to his 'humblest but also most constant teacher' is made in the lecture 'A Greek – Makriyannis' [*Enas Ellinas – o Makriyannis*, 1943] reprinted in the *Essays* (first volume), where the comparison with the painter Theophilos, originally from

Seferis' native Smyrna, is emphasised. There is also in the first volume of the *Essays* his lecture of 1947 on Theophilos. This and the essay on Makriyannis have been translated by Rex Warner and Th. D. Frangopoulos in Seferis, *On the Greek Style: Selected Essays in Poetry and Hellenism* (London, 1967). *The Memoirs of General Makriyannis 1797–1864* have been edited and translated by H. A. Lidderdale (London, 1966). Seferis records his emotion on reading the first lines of Prometheus in his diary, *Days*, volume IV (*Meres D'*, Athens, 1977); it is the entry for an undated Sunday in August 1941. He returns to this memory and to his feeling for the Greek light in *Days*, volume V (Wednesday, 12 February 1947).

Pound speaks of 'mists and fogs since the nineties' in 'The Later Yeats', 1914 (*Literary Essays*, 1954; paperback edn., London, 1960), where he reviews the verse collection by Yeats, *Responsibilities*. His famous warning of the consequences 'when the application of word to thing goes rotten' was made in 'How to Read', 1928. (*op.cit*). Eliot's address, 'The Social Function of Poetry' was first given in 1943, developed for a French audience in 1945, and published in his book *On Poetry and Poets* (London, 1957). The lines from Daniel's poem, 'To his Reader', are quoted from *The Oxford Book of Sixteenth Century Verse*, ed. E. K. Chambers (Oxford, 1932).

Wordsworth states the necessity for 'every great Poet [. . .] before he can be thoroughly enjoyed [. . .] to call forth and communicate *power*' in his 'Essay, Supplementary to the Preface' to *Poems* (1815). Hazlitt takes up the idea in his essay of 1818 'On Poetry in General'. His preoccupation (and that of other romantics) with this theme is discussed by John Kinnaird in *William Hazlitt: Critic of Power* (New York, 1941). Thomas De Quincey follows him in 'Letters to a Young Man Whose Education has been Neglected', 1823. Nadezhda Mandelstam tells of her husband's comment to Akhmatova, 'Poetry is power', in Chapter 37, 'The Changes of Values', in *Hope Against Hope* (London, 1971). Akhmatova's poem 'Voronezh' was written in March 1936, and first published (without the four-line coda) in 1940. The full version appeared in the last collection of her poems to come out during Akhmatova's life, *The Flight of Time* (*Beg vremeni*, Moscow and Leningrad, 1965). She had recited it in full to Lydia Chukovskaya in March 1958 as the latter relates in her second book of memoirs about the poet (*Zapiski ob Anne Akhmatovoy* II, Paris, 1980, under date 26 March). The celebration at the close of the poem seems to allude to Peter's revelling as described in the Third Canto of his narrative poem *Poltava* (1828–29), and similar feasting is evoked in a lyric of 1835, 'The Feast of Peter I' [*Pir Petra pervogo*]. Pushkin's 'vault of pale green' has its place in the little poem of 1828 on St Petersburg 'Splendid city, wretched city' [*Gorod pyshnyy, gorod bednyy*].

Viktor Frank's examination of the writer's role in Russia as the true voice of conscience was made in an article on Pasternak's death, first published in *The Dublin Review* (Autumn, 1960). A Russian translation, *'Delo sovesti'* [A Matter of Conscience] is included in his *Selected Essays* (*Izbrannye stat'i*, London, 1974).

Yeats expressed his disapproval of the First World War poets who chose passive suffering as their theme in the Introduction to his *Oxford Book of Modern Verse 1892–1935* (Oxford, 1936).

Pasternak commented on Akhmatova's 'purity of attention' to Tsvetaeva in 1922, as she reminds him in a letter of 29 June in that year. See her *Unpublished Letters* (*Neizdannye pis'ma*, Paris, 1972). Ezra Pound's 'The Serious Artist' is among his *Literary Essays* cited above. Octavio Paz wrote on Solzhenitsyn in *PN Review* 1 (volume 4, number 1 of *Poetry Nation*).

2. *The nature and validity of poetic witness*

The 'almost pathological' timidity of Cavafy is recorded by J. A. Sareyannis in 'What Was Most Precious – His Form' (*Grand Street*, New York, Vol. 2, No. 3, Spring 1983). On Cavafy's truthfulness as an artist Seferis wrote in the long article, 'A Few

References

Things More Concerning the Alexandrian' (*Akomi liga gia ton Alexandrino*, 1941–6), included in *Essays I*.

Mandelstam's figure of the Chinese junks is used in the first section of his *Conversation about Dante* (*Razgovor o Dante*, 1933). This has been translated by Clarence Brown and Robert Hughes, whose version is reprinted in Osip Mandelstam, *Selected Essays* tr. Sidney Monas (Austin and London, 1977). Jane Garey Harris presents her translation, which includes addenda from Mandelstam's first draft, in *The Complete Critical Prose and Letters*, edited by her, and with translations also by Constance Link (Ann Arbor, 1979). He wrote about the poet's rightness in 'The Morning of Acmeism' (*Utro akmeizma*, written 1913, published 1919). The lines on silent work silvering the plough and the versifier's voice were written in 1937 during his last months at Voronezh. It was Ilya Selvinsky who claimed the poet is always right (see Lazar Fleishman, *Boris Pasternak v tridtsatye gody*, Jerusalem, 1984, note on p. 333). Yury Tynyanov's remarks on the ethical basis of modern poetry are to be found at the close of his essay 'About Khlebnikov' (*O Khlebnikove*, 1928), reprinted in the *Collected Works* (*Sobranie sochineniy Velimira Khlebnikova*, 4 vols, Moscow, 1928–1933, reissued Munich 1968–71).

Dorothy Wordsworth describes the meeting with the leech-gatherer in her *Journal* (3 October 1800). Wordsworth predicts the time when he 'may scarcely see at all' in Book XI of the 1805–6 *Prelude*, 11.338f.

Eliot wrote on the last canto of the *Paradiso* in his essay on Dante (1929, republished in *Selected Essays*). His statement that 'the great poet, in writing himself, writes his time' appeared in 'Shakespeare and the Stoicism of Seneca' (1927, also in *Selected Essays*). On private experience that can express 'the despair of a generation', he spoke in his broadcast of 1951 'Virgil and the Christian World', republished in the book *On Poetry and Poets*. His description of *The Waste Land* as 'rhythmical grumbling' is placed as the epigraph on p. 1 of Valerie Eliot's facsimile edition of the poem (London,

1971). Henry James's consternation on the outbreak of the Great War is amply witnessed in his letters during the first weeks of hostilities. The quotation here is from one to Rhoda Broughton (10 August 1914).

Pasternak's statement 'The aim of creating is the giving of oneself' [*Tsel' tvorchestva – samootdacha*] is made in a poem of 1956, 'Fame is an unlovely thing' [*Byt' znamenitym – nekrasivo*]. Mrs Mandelstam finds fault with his use of the word 'creating' as pretentious in *Hope Abandoned* (Ch. 30, v 'Poetic Recognition', London, 1974), and criticises his notion of 'giving oneself'. Blok's belief that a poet's 'passion' is 'steeped in the spirit of the age' he affirms in the essay on Catiline (*Katilina*, April – May, 1918). On the importance of a poet preserving his own rhythm he wrote in 'The Writer's Nature' (*Dusha pisatelya*, 1909). He accepted the role of witness to 'a great epoch' in the Notebook entry, already referred to, for 14 April 1917. On 23 June he wrote in his Diary: 'I have only a view, but no voice (feeling).' On 29 January 1918, the day after completing *The Twelve*, he put down in his Notebook, '*Today I am a genius*' (his italics). He had referred to the Rasputin within himself in his Diary for 13 July 1917; the reference to 'the fogs of anarchism and bolshevism' is recorded there on 30 July. His claim to have 'simply stated a fact' about the appearance of Christ in the blizzard of *The Twelve* was made in his diary on 10 March 1918. His reading of Renan's *Vie de Jésus* is recorded in a Notebook entry (7 January 1918). The essay of March – April 1918 'The Collapse of Humanism' [*Krushenie gumanizma*] contains his statement on the necessity of 'a *tragic* outlook' (his italics) for understanding the world.

Mandelstam wrote of *The Twelve* in his essay on Blok 'The Badger's Lair' (*Barsuch'ya nora*, 1922), which makes favourable mention of Viktor Zhirmunsky's short study, *The Poetry of Aleksandr Blok* (*Poeziya Aleksandra Bloka*, 1922; facsimile edn., Letchworth, 1975). Sergey Hackel examines the whole context of *The Twelve* in *The Poet and the Revolution* (Oxford, 1975). On

References

Blok's interest in the writings of Vladimir Solovyov, see Avril Pyman's *The Life of Aleksandr Blok*: Vol. I *The Distant Thunder* (Oxford, 1979), where it is discussed in Ch. IV, 'The Covenant'.

Yeats's declaration on tragic insight as the first step in living appears in *The Trembling of the Veil*, Book I, XXI (1922; collected in *Autobiographies*, London, 1926). He affirms 'We were the last romantics' in the poem 'Coole Park and Ballylee, 1931'. His 'ancestral stair' trodden by Goldsmith and the others is celebrated in 'Blood and the Moon'; compare 'The Seven Sages', in the same volume *The Winding Stair and Other Poems*, 1933. 'High Talk' is the title of one of his *Last Poems*, which begins: 'Processions that lack high stilts have nothing that catches the eye'. He wrote of 'the one Irish century that escaped from darkness and confusion' in the Introduction to his play *The Words upon the Window-Pane* (1930; publ. 1934). The little poem 'To be Carved on a Stone at Thoor Ballylee' opens with the words 'I, the poet William Yeats'. He speculates on his share of responsibility for the Dublin riots in another chapter of *The Trembling of the Veil* – 'The Stirring of the Bones', and asks the question about the effect of his play *Cathleen ni Houlihan* (1902), in which Maud Gonne played the title role, upon those who led the Easter rising of 1916, in 'The Man and the Echo' (*Last Poems*). His definition of rhetoric as 'the will trying to do the work of the imagination' appears in an essay of 1903, 'Emotion of Multitude', included in *Ideas of Good and Evil* (1896–1903), and subsequently in his *Essays and Introductions* (London, 1961).

Eliot's 1940 lecture on Yeats is in *On Poetry and Poets*. C. H. Sisson's article 'W. B. Yeats' (1970) has been republished in the collection of his essays edited by Michael Schmidt, *The Avoidance of Literature* (Manchester, 1978).

Conor Cruise O'Brien's essay 'Yeats and Fascism' appears in his book *Excited Reveries* (London, 1965). The passage to which I refer is quoted by Michael Hamburger in Ch. 5, 'Absolute Poetry and Absolute Politics', in *The Truth of Poetry* (London, 1969; with postscript, Manchester, 1932).

References

Pound's *Pisan Cantos* (LXXIV to LXXXIV inclusive) were completed in 1948 (publ. London, 1949). The passage on Ford's and Yeats's conversational powers is in Canto LXXXII; he confesses to have been 'hard as youth' in Canto LXXX, and to having shown not enough pity in Canto LXXVI; and describes himself as 'a man on whom the sun has gone down' in Canto LXXIV. The lyrical passage 'What thou lov'st well' closes Canto LXXXI. The implied comparison with Herakles in the passage quoted from Canto CXVI (*Drafts and Fragments*, London, 1970) becomes clear from his translation of Sophocles' *Women of Trachis*, 1956 (paperback edn., London, 1969), when Herakles, in what Pound considered to be 'the key phrase, for which the play exists', calls out

> Come at it that way, my boy, what
> SPLENDOUR,
> IT ALL COHERES.

Pound's admission that he had 'come too late to the consciousness of doubt' is quoted by Donald Davie in the Introduction to *Pound* (Modern Masters, London, 1975). Eliot speaks of his unselfish service to art in the Introduction to Pound's *Critical Essays*. The poet whose 'zeal for what he called and thought liberty' in religion and politics Samuel Johnson discounted in appraising his work was Akenside (*Lives of the Poets*, Oxford, 1905, vol. III).

3. *Isolation and community*

Montale's 'The Solitude of the Artist' (*La Solitudine dell' artista*, 1952) was published in his *Auto da fé* (Milan, 1966). Arshi Pipa reprints it in *Montale and Dante* (Minneapolis, 1968), together with the 'imaginary interview' called 'Intentions' (*Intenzioni*, 1946; amended, 1961). Both have an English translation accompanying the text. Montale refers to living under a glass bell in the latter essay. Tsvetaeva's proposition is to be found in her essay 'Epic and Lyric in Contemporary Russia' (*Epos i lirika v sovremennoy Rossii*, 1932), reprinted in her *Selected Prose* (*Izbrannaya proza v dvukh tomakh*, New York, 1979, II).

'Civilization – spurns – the Leopard!' is the opening line of a poem by Emily Dickinson dated 'about 1862' by T. H. Johnson in his edition of the *Poems*, vol. I, (Cambridge, Mass., 1958). Tsvetaeva describes herself as a captive lion in 'Homesickness' [*Toska po rodine* . . .], a poem of 1934. Mandelstam compares his position with that of an *edinolichnik* in 'Stanzas' (*Stansy*, May – June 1935). On the ambivalences of this poem see Jennifer Baines, *Mandelstam: The Later Poetry* (Cambridge, 1976, pp. 127–32). Emily Dickinson refers to 'the Amherst heart' in a letter of 1886 to J. K. Chickering, quoted in Jay Leyda's *Years and Hours of Emily Dickinson*, vol. II (New Haven, 1960). Her letter to Higginson about the lexicon was written in April 1862. Allen Tate's essay of 1932 on Emily Dickinson is reprinted in his book *The Man of Letters in the Modern World: Selected Essays: 1928–1935* (New York, 1955).

Tsvetaeva writes of her 'principal soul' as being German in 'About Germany: extracts from a diary of 1919' (*O Germanii: vyderzhki iz dnevnika 1919 goda*, first publ. 1925, reprinted in *Selected Prose* I). She refers to 'the pliancy of the Russian tongue' in the sixth poem of the cycle addressed to Mandelstam, 'Verses on Moscow' [*Stikhi o Moskve*, 1916]. Brodsky's fine essay 'The Poet and Prose' [*Poet i proza*] is the Foreword to Tsvetaeva's *Selected Prose*. The lines he quotes about the poet and his speech are at the beginning of a sequence of three lyrics entitled '*The Poet*' (*Poet*, 1923). The poem by Rilke is 'The Reader', (*Der Lesende*, 1901, from *Das Buch der Bilder*, 1902), which Pasternak translated in his *Autobiographical Sketch* (*Avtobiograficheskiy ocherk*, 1957). Tsvetaeva wrote about her difficulties over finding an audience in her article, 'The Poet and Time' (*Poet i vremya*, 1932, also in *Selected Prose* I).

Lawrence's review of *In The American Grain* (1926) is reprinted in *Phoenix* (London, 1936). Lowell's essay on Williams has been cited above (notes to Ch. 1). Eliot speaks of 'the mind of Europe' in 'Tradition and the Individual Talent' (1919), republished in *Selected Essays*, and there too advances his idea of 'depersonalisation'. His 'Puritan prejudices' in relation to Goethe are discussed by Mario Praz in 'T. S. Eliot as a Critic', included by Allen Tate in the collection of essays *T. S. Eliot: The Man and his Work* (1966; London, 1967).

Yeats wrote about 'a community bound together by imaginative possessions' in 'The Galway Plains' (1903), where he also mentions Raftery the blind poet (1784–1834) who chanted his verses in Gaelic. The essay forms part of *Ideas of Good and Evil* (1903), and is republished in his *Essays and Introductions* (London, 1961). He accepts the studio and the drawing-room as 'a true theatre of beauty' in 'Certain Noble Plays of Japan' (1916), also in *Essays and Introductions*.

Seferis prefaced his translation of *The Waste Land* [*I Erimi Khora*], accompanied by 'The Hollow Men', 'Marina' and 'Difficulties of a Statesman', with an 'Introduction to T. S. Eliot' (*Eisagogi ston Th. S. Eliot*, 1936), which opens the first volume of the *Essays*. He published a translation of *Murder in the Cathedral* [*Foniko stin Ekklesia*] in 1963. His essay 'C. P. Cavafy, T. S. Eliot: A Comparison' (*K. P. Kavafis, Th. S. Eliot: paralliloi*, 1946) is also in the first volume; the second contains his 'Letter to a Foreign Friend' [*Gramma s' enan xeno filo*], contributed to *T. S. Eliot, A Symposium*, ed. R. March and Tambimuttu (London, 1949), and also 'T. S. E. Pages from a Diary' (*Th. S. E: selides apo ena imerologio*, 1965). The first and the second of these have been translated in Seferis, *On the Greek Style* (see notes to Ch. 1). His remark on the 'tone of senility' in Eliot and Cavafy belongs to 'A Few Things More Concerning the Alexandrian' (see above, note to Ch. 2). There too he remarks on Cavafy's isolation, and his lack of a natural gift for language. Seferis first saw the low coastline of Alexandria on 16 May 1941, when he recorded in his diary the under-

References

standing of Cavafy it gave him. This passage is repeated in 'A Few Things More . . .' The essay begins with the picture of Cavafy in his 'half-lit library'. Cavafy's distinction is between *Ellin* and *Ellinikos*, as reported by Seferis in the essay that compares him with Flaubert. There his remark on being an historical poet is recorded: 'I should never have been able to write fiction or drama,' he said towards the end of his life, 'but I feel within me 125 voices that say I would have been able to write history'. Seferis discusses Cavafy's 'special demotic' when considering the famous poem 'Ithaca' (*Ithaki*, 1911) in 'A Few Things More . . .' Montale's comment on Cavafy is quoted by Sereni in an essay about the latter, 'The Statue that Moved' (*La statua che s'è mossa*, 1956) reprinted in *Gli immediati dintorni*. Milosz places his tribute to Cavafy at the climax of his final lecture, 'On Hope'.

The lines by Wordsworth on Newton's statue in Trinity College chapel did not have the two from which my quotation was taken in the 1805–6 version. The full form appears in the 1850 Prelude, Book III, 60–3. He speaks of the Poet's part in welcoming science to 'the household of man' in his Preface to *Lyrical Ballads, with Pastoral and Other Poems* (1802). Dante meets Cacciaguida in a central episode of the *Paradiso* (Cantos XV–XVII). The celebration of Florence in its antique simplicity belongs to Canto XV. The expression 'nameless names' is borrowed from *The Dunciad* (1743), Bk III, 1.157.

Machado's *Juan de Mairena* (1936) has been translated by Ben Belitt (Berkeley and Los Angeles, 1963). His comment on the *romances* is made in the *Prologue* to the 1917 edition of *Campos de Castilla*. Gogol's admiration for Russian popular speech is expressed at the end of ch. 5 in *Dead Souls* (*Myortvye dushi*, 1842). Andrey Sinyavsky bears witness to its continuing vitality, as he encountered it when a political prisoner, in his book (under the pseudonym 'Abram Terz') *A Voice from the Chorus* (*Golos iz khora*, London, 1973).

The definition of a national language, and the claim that the

Greeks had done uniquely well in preserving theirs against all odds, appear in the same paragraph of Seferis' brief statement, 'An Example' (*Ena paradeigma*, 1946), in the first volume of his *Essays*. The observation about the advantages of illiteracy for the understanding of poetry is made in his 'Introduction to T. S. Eliot', and may have been suggested by Eliot's definition of his preferred audience for the plays in *The Use of Poetry* [...] quoted earlier in this chapter.

It is extraordinary that Tsvetaeva's response to the Russian language should have remained as fresh as ever, despite separation from her homeland. She wrote less verse in the 1930s, but this was only, as she explains, because the émigré editors were readier to publish her prose, and household cares did not allow the leisure for concentrating on poetic composition. Her letter to Anna Tesková, her Czech friend, of 24 November 1933, makes these points. It is published in *Pis'ma k Anne Teskovoy* (Prague, 1969). David Bethea in *Khodasevich: His Life and Art* (Princeton, 1983) quotes from the latter's essay 'Literature in Exile' (*Literatura v izgnanii*, 1933), republished in Khodasevich, *Literaturnye stat'i i vospominaniya* ed. N. Berberova (New York, 1954), and also from the essay on *Pan Tadeusz* (1934). Berberova records the desperate cry of Khodasevich 'Here, I cannot [...] live and write [...]' in her memoirs *The Italics are Mine* (New York, 1969; authorised translation from the original, *Kursiv moy* (Munich, 1972)). Vladimir Nabokov's Russian translation of *Lolita* (London, 1967) was published twelve years after the original first came out.

Mandelstam's poem 'I look frost in the face, alone' [*V litso morozu ya glyazhu odin*] was written in January 1937, and the second poem from which I quote [*Kuda mne det'sya v etom yanvare?*] was finished on 1 February of the same year. On 21 January he wrote to Tynyanov about the fact that 'lately' he had 'become intelligible positively to all'.

References

4. The international code of poetry

Volapük had a very large number of adherents in the 1880s until Esperanto appeared at the end of the decade. Mandelstam uses the Russian word in an essay of 1923, 'Notes on Poetry' (*Zametki o poezii*), when he speaks of 'newspaper gibberish' (*volapyuk gazety*). Eliot's statement that 'genuine poetry can communicate before it is understood' is made in his essay on the *Inferno* ('Dante', 1929). He returns to the topic in 'The Social Function of Poetry' (cited above in notes to Ch. 1). The 'auditory imagination' is defined in *The Use Of Poetry* [. . .] where he discusses Arnold. He writes of the dead poets asserting their immortality in 'Tradition and the Individual Talent'. His remark on poetry being 'stubbornly national' occurs in 'The Social Function of Poetry', where he speaks of its unique value for 'the people of the poet's race and language'. What he means by Dante's '*visual* imagination' (his italics) is explained in the essay on the *Inferno*.

Walter Benjamin's essay 'The Task of the Translator' (introducing a translation of Baudelaire's *Tableaux parisiens*) is published in *Illuminations*, tr. H. Zohn (London, 1970; paperback edn., 1973). Khlebnikov's poem 'A Discourse on L' [*Slovo o el'*] was not published until 1920; the elucidatory prose essay, which has the provisional title 'Breaking Down of the Word', was written in 1915–16. Tynyanov's comment on the new relationships between words explored or created by Khlebnikov occurs in his essay on the latter cited in notes to Ch. 2. His discussion of Pasternak in 'The Interval' (*Promezhutok*, 1924) has been translated as 'Pasternak's "Mission" ' by the editors in *Pasternak: Modern Judgements* ed. Donald Davie and Angela Livingstone (London, 1969). Mandelstam's comparison of Khlebnikov to a mole comes in the essay 'On the Nature of the Word' (*O prirode slova*, 1922). His comments on the Italian language were made in the *Conversation about Dante*, cited in notes to Ch. 2. On poetry breaking down national frontiers he wrote in 'Notes on Chénier' (*Zametki o Shen'e*, 1914 or 1915? publ.

109

References

1928), and on poetry as a plough in 'The Word and Culture' (*Slovo i kul'tura*, 1921). He connects Verlaine with Villon in his essay 'François Villon' (*Fransua Villon*, 1910, publ. 1913), and Dante with Rimbaud in the fifth section of his *Conversation about Dante*. His poem 'To the German Language' [*K nemetskoy rechi*] is dated August 1932.

Brodsky describes Tsvetaeva as 'the most interesting thinker of her time' in the Foreword to her *Selected Prose*, cited in notes to Ch. 3. His remark on each word as the beginning of thought for a poet is quoted from the brilliant long disquisition 'About a Poem (In lieu of a Foreword)' [*Ob odnom stikhotvorenii* (*Vmesto predisloviya*)] prefacing vol. I of her 'Lyrics and Long Poems' (*Stikhotvoreniya i poemy*, New York, 1980). Tsvetaeva's essay 'The Cedar: An Apology (On Prince S. Volkonsky's Book *Motherland*)' (*Kedr: Apologiya. (O Knige Kn. S. Volkonskogo 'Rodina'*), 1923) is republished in *Selected Prose* I. Her essay 'The Poet and Time' (*Poet i vremya*, 1932) is in the same volume.

Robert Frost's views on sentence sounds, taken from a letter to John T. Bartlett, are quoted from *Modern Poets on Modern Poetry* ed. James Scully (London, 1966).

On Pasternak's translations from Tabidze, and Tabidze's satisfaction with them, G. Tsurikova has written in her introductory essay 'The Poetry of Titsian Tabidze' [*Poeziya Titsiana Tabidze*] to Tabidze's *Lyrics and Long Poems* in translation (*Stikhotvoreniya i poemy*, Moscow and Leningrad, 1964). Pasternak mentions Keats and Swinburne in 'Notes of a Translator' (*Zametki perevodchika*, 1944). *The Correspondence of Boris Pasternak and Olga Freidenberg* (New York and London, 1982) has been translated by Elliott Mossman and Margaret Wettlin; Mossman edited the Russian text, *Boris Pasternak: Perepiska s Ol'goy Freydenberg* (New York and London, 1981).

Patrick Boyde comments on the opening lines of the *Paradiso* in *Dante, Philomythes and Philosopher: Man in the Cosmos* (Cambridge, 1981).

References

Arnold attributes to the 'rare excellence of the great style' in poetry 'influences of refining and elevation' in his address of 1888, 'Milton', published in *Essays in Criticism: Second Series* (London, 1888). His General Introduction to T. H. Ward's *The English Poets* (1880), reprinted as 'The Study of Poetry' in *Essays in Criticism: Second Series*, concludes with his reliance on 'the instinct of self-preservation in humanity', and the phrase is used again in 'Literature and Science', the second of his three *Discourses in America* (London, 1889). Nadezhda Mandelstam speaks of poetry as a 'golden treasury' of values in *Hope Against Hope*, Ch. 71 'Rebirth'. On the crucial importance of memory see her chapter on that subject, No. 18 of *Hope Abandoned* (London, 1974). I quote Laura Riding Jackson's strictures on the harm done by poetry from Michael Hamburger's *The Truth of Poetry* (cited in notes to Ch. 2 above) from which the remark of Różewicz is also taken. Zbigniew Herbert's appears in the interview republished in *PN Review* 26 (vol. 6, no. 6). Sinyavsky's comment on *samizdat* is made in his celebrated essay 'The Literary Process in Russia' (*Literaturnyy protsess v Rossii*, publ. in *Kontinent* I, 1974; tr. Michael Glenny in *Kontinent* I, English version, London 1976). Machado writes on Shakespeare in *Juan de Mairena* (1936), section XLV. On chronological periods and the apocalyptic vision see Frank Kermode's *The Sense of an Ending* (New York, 1967).

111

POETRY IN A DIVIDED WORLD

POETRY
IN A DIVIDED
WORLD

The Clark Lectures 1985

HENRY GIFFORD

Emeritus Professor of English and Comparative Literature
University of Bristol

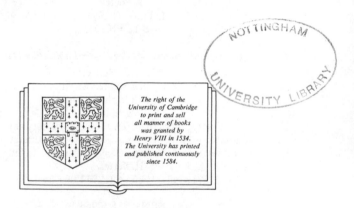

The right of the
University of Cambridge
to print and sell
all manner of books
was granted by
Henry VIII in 1534.
The University has printed
and published continuously
since 1584.

CAMBRIDGE UNIVERSITY PRESS

Cambridge
London   New York   New Rochelle
Melbourne   Sydney

Published by the Press Syndicate of the University of Cambridge
The Pitt Building, Trumpington Street, Cambridge CB2 1RP
32 East 57th Street, New York, NY 10022, USA
10 Stamford Road, Oakleigh, Melbourne 3166, Australia

First published 1986

Printed in Great Britain at
the University Press, Cambridge

British Library Cataloguing in Publication Data
Gifford, Henry
Poetry in a divided world.—(The Clark
lectures; 1985)
1. Poetry
I. Title II. Series
808.1 PN1031

Library of Congress Cataloguing in Publication Data
Gifford, Henry.
Poetry in a divided world.
(The Clark lectures; 1985)
Bibliography; p.
1. Poetry, Modern—20th century—History and
criticism—Addresses, essays, lectures. 2. Literature
and society—Addresses, essays, lectures. I. Title.
II. Series.
PN1271.G47 1986 821'.914'09 85-18988

ISBN 0 521 30944 1

GG